*The
House Was
Quiet and the
World Was
Calm*

Helen Bevington

The House Was Quiet and the World Was Calm

Harcourt Brace Jovanovich, Inc.
New York

First edition

ISBN 0-15-142190-0

Library of Congress Catalog
Card Number: 74-134570

Printed in the United States of America

A B C D E

Most of all for Philip

"The house was quiet because it had to be. . . .
And the world was calm."
> —From a title poem by Wallace Stevens

" 'Ah,' he said at death, 'so this world is not
made for me and this house is not mine.' "
> —From Camus, *Notebooks*

*The
House Was
Quiet and the
World Was
Calm*

REPORT FROM THE CAROLINAS

It's a debatable land. The winds are variable,
Especially winds of doctrine—though the one
Prevailing breeze is mild, we say, and southerly.
We have a good deal of sun,

And our peach trees bloom too early. The first light
    promise
Is lightly kept in a Carolina spring
(It blows both hot and cold). Yet by February
There is the flowering

Of yellow jasmine and sudden gold forsythia,
And the mockingbirds—at night the threat of snow.
Northerners passing on their way to Florida
Say it's not Florida, though,

This in-between land. There's the coastal region,
For instance, next a calm sea. Yet too near
Are the dangerous shoals, outlying and inhospitable.
Out there you find Cape Fear.

There's the Piedmont, where I live, the plateau uprising
Between high Appalachians and the sea.
It would seem a temperate world. We take things easy.
Our ways are leisurely,

And people tend to speak to one another,
Observing the civilities. Seldom heard

Is bitter rebel talk now, seldom "Damnyankee,"
At least not as one word.

And everyone is a Democrat, almost,
Though argumentative. Not a few incline
Toward oratory still, being Southern orators.
Our grapes are muscadine.

Our works are amiable. We grow camellias
In April gardens, we love azalea flowers.
Both the Carolina wren and Whistler's mother
Are specialties of ours.

We have quail in the yard and dogwood in the woodlands,
A skyful of buzzards, the wisteria trees,
The pines, the magnolias. Also we have lately
Certain uncertainties

(I speak as a country person), for winds are variable,
Especially winds of change. From freezing springs
To summer drought, knowing these fluctuations,
We fear for other things.

The danger is, one becomes a little provincial,
Too quick to see as a microcosm this
Mid-country where one lives, this red-clay country,
An odd antithesis,

Where the apricot flowers too soon and the mimosa
Blooms endlessly; where now, in the sunstrewn days,
The hydrogen bomb is ours, in all the seasons—
Another crop to raise.

And nobody says, of the bomb site down by Ellenton,
That winds are gathering there, or that on the whole
They threaten ill. Yet, in the imagination,
Fear is another shoal.

I

⟫⟫⟫⟫⟫⟫⟫⟫⟫⟫⟫⟫⟫⟫⟪⟪⟪⟪⟪⟪⟪⟪⟪⟪⟪⟪⟪⟪

"It is not Eden," said Jonathan Daniels about the state of
North Carolina, thus gallantly yielding a point. I would
make the same concession: it is not Eden. When I came in
my thirties to live in North Carolina, it was a distant and
alien land—the South—where I had never been or wanted
to be. No ancestor of mine was born here or buried in this
ground. None presumably set foot here, except those sent
down to subdue the rebels. They fought on the Yankee side.

Yet one of its towns is named Welcome, another Heartsease. Charity greets you in its name. So does Whynot, N. C.
When Lord Cornwallis passed by in an April spring during
an earlier war, on his way to defeat at Yorktown, he called
North Carolina "a damned hornet's nest." That is not a
typical view. It is generally agreed to have better manners,
a temperate, hospitable state of tobacco barns and china-
berry trees, red clay and hot sun, cardinals and mockingbirds, black-eyed peas and hush puppies, with its own history
of heroes like Andrew Johnson and Evangelist Billy Graham,
its own fame as the birthplace of the airplane, Virginia Dare,
and Whistler's mother—all three of whom have miraculously
survived their birth. The flying machine, airborne on the
Outer Banks in 1903, continues to fly. Virginia Dare, who

at nine days old disappeared from the face of the earth in 1587, is now performing nightly in "The Lost Colony." Whistler's mother became an "Arrangement in Grey and Black, No. 1" in 1872.

Out in the western hills, they still play the dulcimer. They take snuff and a few handle rattlesnakes at revival meetings. Till recently we had "white supremacy" and Jim Crow: whites, blacks, and Cherokee Indians.

I came during yet another war, the worst so far, World War II, in a real sense fleeing a threatened city and (as if one could) a threatened planet. The American forces were fighting the Japanese on Guadalcanal, Hitler had launched a desperate offensive against Stalingrad, when on an August morning in 1942 we jumped into the car and drove away from one lifetime in New York, B. and I, with the two boys in the back seat and a feeling of narrow escape in our hearts. How many lives had we left to live? New York was peaceless, a city to unlearn. The war had taught us to expect calamity.

As we crossed the George Washington Bridge to New Jersey looking back on a clear day at the downtown skyscrapers, not yet bombed but perishable, the fate of these steel pinnacles as targets written in the sky, I thought of George S. Kaufman's line: "They say there'll be palm trees someday where the Empire State Building is." New York and we were still intact and vertical, thank God, and about to part.

I sat in the front seat beside B., holding the road map and a book of coupons issued for gas rationing. We had five hundred miles to go to a new existence and barely enough gasoline stamps to take us there. We might be stranded halfway. Somewhere in New Jersey B. made a sharp turn to the right.

"Stop, you're on the wrong road!" I cried. "Where on earth are you going?"

"I saw a sign back there to Princeton," he said.

"*Princeton!*" I said. "Darling, they don't want us at Princeton. You've been hired to teach at Duke, remember? Duke University. It's in North Carolina."

"I know, I remember."

"Well, turn around then. You're using up precious gas. You're going in the wrong direction!"

"I want the boys to see Princeton."

"*Why*, heaven forbid?"

"It has a beautiful campus."

At that I began to yell. "Stop the car! I mean it, *stop* the car!"

"What's the matter with you?"

"I'm getting out."

"Where do you think you're going?"

"I'm going to walk to North Carolina."

So we backed around, and later there was another hassle over a side trip to visit Thomas Jefferson and the University of Virginia. By evening we drove up Main Street, Durham, seeking a university of our own, a white house as well—one we had rented yesterday sight unseen by telephone from New York.

We found the house first, a small white frame cottage in Tuscaloosa Forest, an outskirt beyond the city limits. Trees sheltered it and green thoughts, a grove of hickories and loblolly pines, with a redbud tree beside the kitchen door.

I had never seen a dwelling so obviously benign, a genial house, well-circumstanced, though the cellar was damp enough that crayfish swam in its calm waters. The reason for its indulgent air was plain: it was psychic. It had precognition and ether waves. An earlier owner had been J. B. Rhine, the parapsychologist at Duke, who left behind an aura of extrasensory perception. To my knowledge there were no actual hovering ghosts or apparitions. During the

7

four years we lived in the house we had nothing to call a psychic experience or visitation, not being receptive to wraiths. But the extrasensory perception testing cards left behind, scattered under the radiators or the kitchen linoleum, gave one a peculiar sense of mind over matter, of divination, even of grace. Besides, the man next door turned out to be a man named Love.

Mr. Love knocked at the door on our arrival to offer his help to get us through the night. What we needed was Love.

"I'm Love," he said modestly, unaware of the broad admission he had made. We hadn't counted on meeting love in the flesh, not so soon, but there he stood—a tall, shy, dark-haired man with a benevolent stoop, polka-dot tie, and Southern accent, who worked understandably enough for the power company. His first name was Roderick.

"It's Love," I said, "we're looking for."

"Yes, ma'am," he said.

The unlocked house was empty save for fifty cardboard cartons of our thousand books. They had been shipped to the University and delivered with dispatch that afternoon. The sight of them distressed Love, not an academic himself but more of a romantic, not convinced as the University clearly was that man can live by books alone. Love's other name was Charity. For our bed of roses, Love even furnished the bed. Excusing himself he hurried over home and returned with two folding cots, blankets, and a gentle Mrs. Love bearing neighborly solicitude. We had come empty-handed to a strange land, but in North Carolina we had found Love.

They lent us dishes, and for the next two weeks we lived without furniture or household goods, since ours had vanished, disappeared without a trace somewhere en route. The war was to blame. It accounted for every shortage or mischance ("There's a war on, you know"), whether the milkman came late or one had lost a furniture van with one's worldly possessions. I didn't mind. I hoped they were permanently lost. It was good to keep house, a clairvoyant house, with nothing in it but bare floors, echoing rooms, and plenty of books to read sitting on the grass.

I was startled by the serenity, fit for such a house. Maybe it *was* hypnotic with occult powers, mystic but not spooked. I listened to the overtones of quiet, trying to grow used to so unnatural a thing as peace of mind, as time for living.

In early September the two boys went up the road a mile to the county school with the charming name of Hope Valley (somehow confused in my memory with Happy Valley, a town in Nevada whose welcoming sign that you pass on the highway says: "HAPPY VALLEY. No services available"). Philip, nine, and David, eleven, started with the same kind of welcome. Because of the difference between a rural Southern school and the only one they had known, the Barnard School in New York, they were well in advance of the students in these large classes. They had looked forward without a qualm to public school in North Carolina. After a day in the seventh grade at Hope Valley, David asked if he could wear overalls and go barefoot. He was urgent about it.

"Why?" I asked.

"To look like the other kids."

"You look all right to me. Do the boys in your class wear overalls?"

"The farm boys do."

The next day he came home beaten up, his face bruised and lips swollen, his clothes dirty and torn. I minded most his frown of bewilderment, the way he stared at nothing.

He threw down his books and his chin trembled. "Tell me," I said.

"During recess. They hit me in the face and knocked me

down. That wasn't so bad, everybody gets socked, but my whole class stood there laughing, all the girls too. They made a circle around me, and every time a girl got a chance she pinched me and kicked me. It was my whole class! Nobody took my side." His voice was incredulous. "I didn't have a single friend."

"What about your teacher?"

"Miss Morris? She was probably watching out the window laughing her head off."

"But, David, it doesn't make sense. Why did it happen? What made them do it to you?"

"They hate me," he said.

"Why, *why* should they hate you?"

"They told me. I'm a Yankee, that's why. They don't want me down here. They hate damnyankees."

"You needn't go back," I said. "We'll find another school."

"I'll go back," he said.

So that was how it was in the South, love and hate together, like any community in the world. It was standardized, the same old fifty-fifty ratio: one horse, one rabbit.

I spent my time that fall, while the hickory trees changed to roofs of gold, writing verse and putting up curtains. On the day the piano tuner came, I was writing a piece about Mr. Love and finishing the curtains for the bathroom.

He was a blind piano tuner, who found his way to our house by bus. While he brought the Knabe up to pitch in the living room, I went to the bathroom, climbed onto the toilet seat, from there to the window sill to hang the curtains. The rod was just beyond reach. As I stood on tiptoe straining with both arms lifted, I listened to him, thinking not of his blindness but of his hearing, the acutely sensitive ears of which he had boasted. I wished my ears were attuned to hearing the right notes, to writing verses about Mr. Love or even love itself. I wished I had good ears. And a delicate tongue.

My foot slipped off the narrow sill. Losing my balance I fell backward, screaming as I went, striking the toilet seat with a clatter and landing with a thud on my bottom on the tile floor. The bathroom curtains covered my head like a shroud.

"Holy, holy, holy!" I groaned, badly shaken up and jolted.

Louder groans came from the door as the frightened piano tuner groped his way in, wringing his hands, his face a picture of horror.

"Oh, lady!" he cried. "I heard a terrific crash in here. Speak to me, lady. Are you hurt? Have you gone and killed yourself?"

I laughed to reassure him. "It's nothing. No harm done."

He stood silent, cocking his head to listen, then heaved a deep sigh. "You don't know what hell I go through," he said. "A blind man alone in the house with a woman, it's double-distilled hell. You hear an awful ruckus, hollering or rattling of pans, and you don't know what they're up to next."

"I'm sorry."

"What happened? Didn't something fall just now?"

"Yes," I said. "I did. I fell off the toilet seat."

He scowled, trying to visualize the scene. "Pardon me," he said hastily and backed out.

A second verse that autumn, "Tar Heel," had to do with the local Dukes. The best line in it, the most impassioned I ever wrote, went straight to the heart of the matter:

My God, the Dukes are everywhere!

However poetical the language, nothing could have been more true. The Dukes were with us in millions and in monument, in the air we breathed. They were in the tobacco smell, the Duke Power Company, Duke Memorial Methodist Church, Duke University, Duke Hospital, Duke Street, Cigarette Street, Duke Forest, the Duke Homestead, the Sarah P. Duke Gardens, the Washington Duke Hotel—in our minds and lives, forever commanding the scene. This was Duke, North Carolina, and I marveled that the town had been too stubborn to change its name. It may have figured it was here first.

Yet Durham had no ante-bellum history, no Old South aristocracy of pillared colonial mansions, cotton plantations, and scattered magnolia blossoms. It had barely an existence till the Civil War ended and two events brought unexpected glory to a hangdog settlement of twenty houses, a general store, a tobacco factory, and two saloons.

The War itself ended here—four miles up the road in Mr. Bennett's farmhouse—when General Johnston surrendered to General Sherman seventeen days after Lee surrendered to Grant (eleven days after the death of Mr. Lincoln), thus bringing about the final collapse of the Confederacy. The War was lost here. Or else it was won, a nation indivisible. Either way you said it, North Carolina had suffered greatly. Nearly one hundred battles or skirmishes were fought on her soil. Her losses in battle exceeded those of any other state, her poverty was intense. In the same year, 1865, Washington Duke returned home from that war with fifty cents to his name and two blind mules.

To start life over at forty-six in a ruined place, with the help of his three sons (Brodie, Ben, and Buck) he made and peddled by wagon drawn by blind mules a smoking tobacco called fancifully, with a fine ring of irony, Pro Bono Publico. It was the rival of Bull Durham. It came from the flue-cured, brightleaf tobacco grown in this countryside, the golden leaf that gleamed into tobacco factories, warehouses, and gold dollars for the Dukes, notably for James B. (Buck), the youngest, most enterprising son.

The daring idea occurred to young Buck Duke of making cigarettes—virtually unknown in America before the Civil War—and, though he despised them himself, of persuading his fellow countrymen to smoke them by the billion. Single-handed, you might say, he gave Americans a taste for self-destruction, changing them into a nation of hooked cigarette smokers.

The poor South. Already guilty of slavery, it became guilty of cigarettes. There were the scaremongers even then who feared these coffin nails and believed tobacco mortally dangerous to health. Others as staunch in support declared that, if breathed into the lungs, it preserved life by destroying the germs of fever and miasma. It lengthened one's days through contentment. It cured headache. When I was a child, I remember, one of the sideshow freaks at the circus would be touted as a cigarette addict, a living skeleton. While he sat on the platform and chain-smoked, we gazed open-mouthed, looking at death in his thin white set face. "He won't live the week out," the barker said.

From this glittering fortune rose Duke University, paved not with gold but with golden tobacco leaves. In 1924, a year before Buck Duke died one of the world's richest men, he bought himself a monument. He offered Trinity College, a little Methodist school off Main Street, a gift of forty-odd millions provided it assume the stature of a university like Yale or Harvard and change its name to Duke.

Buck Duke never went to college and was glad of it, a ruthless self-made man. "If I amount to anything in this world," he said, "I owe it to my daddy and the Methodist Church." He had no need to read books—witness his prodigious wealth—but apparently some people had. If they wanted an education, they might avail themselves in his name of whatever good came of book learning.

The Trinity campus, rebuilt, became the Woman's College. Its redbrick buildings in the style of American Georgian (domes, columns, porticoes, arcades, and chastity lights) made a gracious Southerly school for young women. There at the traffic circle the old father, Wash Duke, sat in a fringed armchair carved in stone and, labeled "Patriot" and "Philanthropist," served as a test of virginity. If he rose and bowed as a girl passed by, that settled it. To such a courtly end had the peddling of tobacco brought him.

Two miles away they cleared a campus for men from a five-thousand-acre forest, erecting Gothic towers, or American Collegiate Gothic towers, that brought the Middle Ages to the middle of North Carolina. The choice was whimsical, of course, in this setting—an architecture of gray stone pinnacles and cloisters, grimly feudal in tone, medieval and monastic—with too little sunlight filtering through the narrow slits of windows. Yet when I first saw its gables and turrets, I felt no shock of surprise, not after the Gothic towers of the University of Chicago where I had gone to school. Mr. Rockefeller's university done in oil and Mr. Duke's university in tobacco looked thoroughly American to me, two lavish monuments to capitalism: rich, gaudy, and familiar, as native as the New York skyscrapers.

The founder's dream included a soaring Chapel, a word too humble for the massive Gothic cathedral that rose skyward and exalted, full of flying buttresses. It seated two thousand, only a trifle smaller than the stadium, glowed with medieval stained glass, and swelled with a tremendous pipe organ that vibrated on the worshiper's breastbone to announce the presence of God. Its bell tower, modeled on Canterbury's, had a carillon of fifty bells to chime "Rock of Ages" over the countryside.

The Chapel lacked only the smell of mortality that marks the true cathedral. It kept no odor of sanctity or whiff of incense; so far it had gathered to itself no candles to the dead. Soon three Dukes lay in state behind a wrought-iron grille in a chapel to the left of the altar—a peculiar way to bury a Methodist. Washington Duke and two of his sons made a strict row, like the tombs of Chartres, each in a sarcophagus under a life-sized effigy in white Carrara marble.

Outside in the quadrangle stood the portly statue of Buck Duke, benefactor in bronze, a cigar held firmly in his left hand ready for a smoke. *The golden weed.*

B. taught English on both East and West Campus, driving hellbent back and forth with a car full of students and twenty minutes between classes to allow him to park and race winded to his classroom. Only the freshmen were isolated in their courses of study by sex. The rest freely mixed and rushed the two miles to and fro, thumbing rides or taking the bus. In his calculations Mr. Duke hadn't reckoned on this basic need of male and female for proximity, three thousand of them determined to walk side by side in the pursuit of love and learning. Had he gone to college, he might have picked up so elementary a fact of education. But it was too late now to rebuild the campuses.

As faculty wife, I seldom saw B.'s academic side, though a little was revealed one Sunday afternoon in November when his freshman girls invited us to tea at Aycock House. They knelt in a solid circle around his chair and gazed spellbound into his eyes, hanging on his words that, I must say, were hardly worth straining oneself to hear. During the social hour, one girl bent her head to notice me sitting, teacup in hand, in complete neglect in an armchair across the parlor. She left his orbit and skipped over for a moment.

"Oh, Mrs. Bevington, how we envy you!" she cried. "It

must be absolute heaven to be married to Dr. Bevington. Do you enjoy him the way we do?"

"No," I said. "But your way is inspiring."

"It surely is," she said. "We surely do experience that man."

The faculty came to call, the wife wearing a hat and white gloves, in a formal visit like a solemn music that we were expected to play back within a week. Lacking a chair in the house or other hospitality, we entertained the first hundred callers standing up, and as the list mounted we grew frantic at the thought of spending the rest of our lives repaying visits. Our guests spoke the official line, divulging nothing in the polite social way, unanimous in praise of the one big happy family that was Duke. One big happy cut-throat family?

"Has the Welcome Wagon visited you yet?" they asked. A wagon, you would think, full of trustees and vice-presidents.

But no revelations. No insights. No gossip. No facts of life. Nothing of birth, copulation, or death.

Each wife admonished me to join something—the Campus Club for faculty wives, the Newcomers Club for new faculty wives, garden clubs, book clubs, travel clubs, discussion clubs, the Tuesday Morning Duplicate Bridge Club, a play-reading group, a Red Cross unit, Civil Defense, P.T.A., and the Needlework Guild. Karate and Yoga came after the war.

The Campus Club met in a downtown mansion, "Four Acres," covering four acres, a former residence of the Dukes. At the head of the stairs, large glass showcases displayed the rich brocaded, bespangled evening dresses worn by the wives of Dukes and those who had intermarried with the Philadelphia Biddles. I attended the opening meeting of the Campus Club, feeling immoral to waste all that daylight, where at three in the afternoon the ladies in the receiving line wore formal evening gowns. (Camus: "Life is too short for afternoon teas.") I went to the Newcomers Club and we played Bingo. After that I stayed home and wrote a verse, "Faculty Wife":

She joins a Club
To read a book.
(Her husband
Has a raveled look.)

To knit, to sing,
Discuss Japan.
(Her husband
Is a lonely man.)

She leads
A Tuesday study group
(His trousers
Have a mournful droop)

On pottery
And Early Glass.
(He walks the Scotty
After class.)

We didn't have a Scotty, nor would B. have walked one anyway. We had a hound dog, Victoria—a bellicose bitch, a disgrace, a scandal—part pointer and part setter with shiny black coat and melting maidenly eyes, who was said to have the makings of a turkey dog. She roamed the neighborhood to bring home dead cats. She chased off the mailman and brawled at the bus stop, teeth bared, to keep the passengers from boarding or leaving the bus. Maybe she thought they were wild turkeys.

More and more, the war grew incredibly far off, in another more ailing and battered world than this, a well-lost world.

We had left disaster behind. We were existing on point rationing beside the still waters.

B. was made air-raid warden of the district. When the sirens sounded the alarm of an evening, he dutifully put on his tin helmet to patrol our meandering rustic lane, Nation Avenue, and the next one to it, Wa-Wa Yonder (not an Indian love call but a Southern name for "way out yonder"), way, way out and by the world forgot, beyond any conceivable place where the German bombs might fall

Instead of bothering with blackout curtains, we switched off the lights till the All Clear came. It seemed a revelation that a few fitful hours of darkness could so change and improve one's life. Sweet was the night air. While the boys read by flashlight under a blanket in their rooms upstairs and the watchdog Victoria slept in a state of beatitude through the sirens, I got acquainted with the night—appareled as it was in the Carolina moon rising locally so luminous, in the white flowering pear tree glowing in spring like a candelabra in the dark. If World War II was one of the first magnitude, so also were the stars.

I had lost fear, not imperturbable but calm. That was the main thing, to feel an unearthly kind of thriving, no longer obsessed by war, listening to the reposeful performance of hoot owls.

The anxiety was missing: this world, this house sheltered from harm. There was the wonderful delusion of peace.

II

>>>>>>>>>>>>>>>>>>>>>>>>>>>>>>>>>

On a morning in October (the second October), Professor Newman White telephoned me to come to his office. He was B.'s chairman, the head of the English Department at Duke, a Shelley scholar. His lifelong passion for Shelley, whom he claimed as spiritual kin, was an endearing thing. More endearing was Newman White himself—a tall, graying, gallant Southerner of infinite kindness, a man of all the virtues. Chaucer's word *gentilesse* should have stayed in the language to describe his worth.

I loved and valued him. The first time we met, he had been skeptical, then surprisingly touched, when I said I had read his enormous two-volume work on Shelley, as few of even his colleagues had done, scholars being classically indifferent to each other's books. Shyly he explained his theory of biography, which went like this:

If you are patient to set down the facts of a man's life, without bias or preconception, he will in the end stand revealed by simply revealing himself. You need not explain or analyze him or interpret his character. No judgment need be made. You have only to state the events tranquil and turbulent by which he is identified: a happy man, a fool, a tragic figure. By the last chapter (unless smothered to death by too much zeal), he will emerge whole, because he cannot help doing so.

This is the case even if the main character happens to be oneself: the portrait is inevitably drawn. Montaigne would have agreed with such a view, the study of *moi-même*, having taken care in his essays to reveal his true proportions: "It is myself that I portray." "I am myself the substance of my book." About Montaigne he was the most learned man alive.

On this October morning, Newman met me at the door and hurried me to a chair beside his desk. He looked so stern I froze like a student summoned for a talking to.

"Will you take over Bev's two freshman courses in the Woman's College?" he asked. "Starting tomorrow morning."

"You mean *teach?*" I said.

"Of course I mean teach."

"You mean teach his *girls?*"

"Naturally."

"Are you firing Bev for misconduct?"

Newman laughed. "It's bad but not that bad," he said. He explained the sudden emergency—a war crisis—caused by the arrival of a large contingent of young recruits for the officers' training program at Duke. The fall term had been under way four weeks. B. was needed on the other campus to teach in that program. His freshman girls were about to lose their man.

I sat stricken at the news, thinking the war crisis was nothing compared to this crisis in my life. I didn't want to teach forty bereft girls who had given their hearts to B. I was licked before I started. It was an unfair assignment. It was calamitous. The girls would mutiny at once. They would make a protest march, with banners, to the Dean's office to demand his immediate return. They would leave school in a body.

"Well?" said Newman, as I hesitated. "It's short notice,

I know, but the situation is desperate. Will you help us out?"

"May I please speak to Bev?" I asked faintly.

"I've already talked it over with him. He thinks it's a great idea," Newman said. "Mind you, I'm not asking you merely to fill in for this school year. I should have said so in the first place. I want you to become a member of the staff as an instructor in English."

That idea had no merit whatever. It alarmed me more than the other, if possible, a step more unnerving. Had they cared to have us both, they would have hired us together. Teachers were one of the latest war shortages, a scarcity like meat and gasoline and butter.

"You don't want two Bevingtons in your department," I said.

"Why not?" said Newman, whose wife was an assistant professor of English.

"I'm one too many."

"Perhaps," said Newman, "perhaps not. Most of the department will undoubtedly think so and resent you as Bev's wife. They will beat their breasts at this appointment and damn me to my face for making it."

"Fine!" I said.

"For some reason," Newman went on, "Duke isn't partial to women teachers. It's prejudiced against them. It believes in a woman's college with men to do the teaching."

"Was that Mr. Duke's view?"

"I doubt it. A number of professors happen to be opposed to women on the faculty, on the grounds they aren't scholars, they're inclined to be flighty and hysterical, domineering, opinionated, trifling by nature, and anyway they belong in the home."

Secretary of Labor Frances Perkins said she found her sex a handicap only in climbing trees. If so, the lady was unique.

"Women marry," said Newman. "They become mothers. They should be content to remain homebodies."

"Where I'm going now—home," I said.

He laughed again his hearty booming laugh. "Before you go, I hope you'll agree to take a chance. It won't be a round of welcoming applause, I grant you. To make things easier, suppose I ask Bev to teach your classes tomorrow and prepare the girls for the switch in instructors."

"I'm not a man, a professor, or a Ph.D.," I said. "I'm a woman. Does he have to tell them that?"

"No," Newman said. "Let them find out for themselves."

I said: "It's bound to be uphill all the way, isn't it?"

When B. came home from school the next afternoon, I asked if he had prepared the girls.

"Certainly," he said. "I told them they had to be nice to you."

"What did they say?"

"Some of them began to cry. They carried on at a great rate, loud lamentation. One girl put her head down on her desk and sobbed 'No, no, *no!*' She's a good student, you'll like her. It was rather moving."

"I'm sorry I missed it."

"If they aren't nice to you, I said, I will come back and wring their little necks."

"You appealed to their patriotism. Accepting me is their supreme sacrifice for the war effort."

"I said it was for God and Uncle Sam."

At the zero hour, I went to class on quivering legs as to a scaffold, before a firing squad. Though I've taught steadily at Duke ever since, any other manner of entering a classroom is a mystery to me. I feel like the man in Belloc's verse:

"My value," William Blood began,
"Is ludicrously small."

Each autumn before the term starts I have the same nightmare, a chimerical dream of walking down the aisle to the lectern and turning in terror to face a roomful of staring eyes. In the accusing silence, while I search through notes that have become blank pages, the students look at the clock, rise from their seats, and speak in unison. "You don't know anything at all!" they say in mournful tones and with bowed heads and muffled tread file slowly out of the classroom.

When the seven sins are counted, I tell myself, there is still the eighth one: ignorance. Chekhov said it in his *Notebooks:* "The university brings out all abilities, including stupidity."

Yet the moment I raised my voice like a gong that morning, the travail was over. Nothing mattered but the business of unfolding the design of the English sentence. By the time I saw B. after class I had changed into the teacher. They were my girls. I began to tell him of the depth of passion roused in me by this new love affair.

"I don't want any salary," I said. "If it likes, the University may have me for nothing. Only let me serve in Mr. Duke's academic grove. I will give myself to the Woman's College, body and soul, all for love."

B. sensed at once the fiddlebrain he had on his hands.

"That's the worst damned rot I've heard yet!" he said in some heat. "Suppose Duke were to take you at your word. You are to be worthy of your hire. You are to be a pearl of great price. Your mind is presumed to be full of golden learning, for which you receive a highly inadequate if not pitiful stipend. Try not to disgrace us both. Try to act, my love, at least gold-plated."

"No need to speak in blank verse," I said. But he was right.

B. taught me other crucial lessons that year. In an age of ungrammarians—those dedicated to imitating the slovenly speech of the man in the street—B. respected grammar for its own sake. He was a real grammarian, who didn't prescribe rules but grasped the splendid logic of construction, the orderly arrangement of words, as God intended, in a reasonable order. When he saw how weak my syntax deplorably was, we spent an evening diagramming the Gettysburg Address. This led to other architectural studies that revealed the building operations of a sentence. I had the time of my life learning from a master builder like him.

Most of all he taught me recognition, and I tried to teach it to my students. "Go ahead, split your infinitives!" I told them peremptorily. "Just be sure you know what an infinitive is. If you must split, split like a lady. Split on purpose!"

I fought an indignant fight against counter words (bartered over the counter) like *outstanding* and *intriguing;* against the murdering of metaphors (getting my back up when the chips were down); against the schoolgirl style and the feminine or hysterical *so.* About the civilities of language, the simple declarative sentence, I grew trumpet-toned. On the virtue of brevity I was long-winded. It exasperated me when they wrote like ribbon clerks or spoke like hillbillies (or sounded like Edmund Spenser, for that matter, in his poetic line: "He, her not finding, both them thus nigh dead did leave"). They were not to feel free to mangle words. Or mince them either.

My girls were gallant and submissive, uncomplaining when I ruled out the Chapel as a subject for freshman themes. The reason: they stared awestruck at the masonry and missed the pigeons. The result: forty identical pieces of gush. Yet the pigeons were not insubstantial. They were no more imaginary than Blake's angels up a tree, "their bright angelic wings bespangling every bough with stars." The birds were on hand cooing overhead, and as somebody (not a student) said of them, they "befouled the steps and an occasional professor." If a student cared to report the scene that reliably, exact in the language of her observing, she was welcome for all of me to undertake an appreciation of the Chapel once a week.

I wanted her to become, like Sir Gawain, courteous in behavior and polished of converse. Like Yeats in his prayer for his daughter, "In courtesy I'd have her chiefly learned." Whether I could teach a student to write was another matter, one that baffled me off and on for years. "Do not try to teach the unteachable to the unteachable," wrote F. L. Lucas, who taught at the University of Cambridge. But what if no such thing existed on either side? Since the question appeared insoluble, the more sporting choice might be to take the opposite view—one can teach anybody anything. How much the learner learned in the process was his problem. The objective, to quote E. E. Cummings, was to proceed, not to succeed.

The next baffling question—could I teach anyone to read? Misinterpretation, said I. A. Richards, is "the normal and probable event." Most people have enough trouble deciphering the words in a newspaper. While we were reading Keats's "On First Looking into Chapman's Homer," a student mistook the title for a baseball term, and the sonnet worked out pretty well that way—Chapman making a home run and Darien a peak, or at least a pitcher's mound, in Connecticut. Robert Frost's "The Oven Bird" they honestly took for a Thanksgiving turkey. What other bird would be found in an oven?

"How much *have* you read?" I asked them. "Make a list of the books you recall reading in the last five years because you wanted to, not for homework." Some fell back on *Christopher Robin*. One peerless girl handed me a list of thirteen typewritten pages and apologized for her bad memory. Another rooted up only two items in her entire reading life, neither one by author or exact title.

I had a perfect confidence, still unshaken, in books. If

you read enough you would reach the point of no return. You would cross over and arrive on the safe side. There you would drink the strong waters and become addicted, perhaps demented—but a Reader.

"Keep track of your reading," I said. "It may turn into the diary of a book and a love affair."

At the end of the year, a few admitted to a newly found rapture for books. "I've got two absolutely favorite authors," a student told me. "They're the same as yours."

"Who are they?"

"Well, you know, Mr. E. B. White. You must be absolutely madly in love with him because you keep going on about him in class."

"He's a good writer, reason enough for love."

"Is he a friend of yours, I mean, you know, personally?"

"No."

"Poor you," she said with sympathy. I felt jilted.

"And who is our other absolutely favorite author?"

"I keep forgetting his name. I think it starts with M."

She must have meant Montaigne.

At least when we were told at examination time to separate the sheep from the goats, I knew the action didn't affect my girls. I had to separate the ewes from the nannies.

The great and abiding danger, without doubt, lay in talking too much. Every teacher does that, accustomed as he is to opening his mouth for fifty minutes and shutting it when the bell rings. All men talk, yes, but not till the bell rings; this distinguishes the teacher from other men. His name is Talkative, "He dwells in Prating Row and is known by the name of Talkative of Prating Row." Yet, as everyone knows, words can bear only so much saying. Fluellen sounded the warning: "So! in the name of Jesu Christ, speak fewer."

If I spoke on, unspent, like an oracle the thunders of

Apollo's word, at least one person in the room lent an attentive ear. Whatever faroff voices the class heeded, I was there to follow the lesson. To teach myself exhausted my vocal cords, but it was a way to learn. At the same time, "Possibly," one had to reflect, "you are something of a bore." Or, as Thurber put it, "You have mislaid your discriminator."

Could I teach myself to teach them? I remember hearing praise of a famed teacher—Gilbert Murray. They said he taught without conceit, taking infinite care to be kind. He taught without the use of scorn. He never made anybody feel like a fool.

"One must not humiliate people," said Chekhov in a letter. "Better to say to a man 'My angel' than hurl 'Fool' at his head, though men are more like fools than they are like angels."

One must not humiliate people, said Camus in his *Notebooks*. "We help a person more by giving him a favorable image of himself than by constantly reminding him of his shortcomings. . . . Do not humiliate him."

"Scorn is contemptible," B. told me, a device of prima donnas and Kittredges. And much too easy. A student was at the mercy of one's rages; in charity leave him untaunted. It required no remarkable talent to be rude with "the insolence of office," to bark, embarrass him before the class, use mockery and wit, even scurrility, at his expense. Or weary him to death. Or ask him to define words like synecdoche, oxymoron, or negative capability.

Why object to his ignorance when without it there would be no need for teachers? A teacher was not a disparager, however well he had trained himself for the task. Not a zealot. Not a moralizer. Not a scold. The greatest praise was approval. The first thing to learn was to listen. Heaven knows one might hear something.

To be honest a few, a slim few, of the answers to teaching were easier to come by than the ones I've mentioned.

"Do you want to know what's wrong with me?" a student asked one day after class. "I haven't grown up."

"It's a common failing."

"What should I do about it?"

"Take the afternoon off," I said, "and outwit youth. Grow up. If that's what you really want, you're practically there."

Whether or not B. took it hard to have a wife entering his profession with both feet, he gave no sign—only love and deliverance. Newman had predicted I would be resented in the department, by some bitterly. And I was. On the first day of teaching, an English professor stopped me in the hall to exclaim, "For the love of God! Is *this* the best Newman could do?"

When I popped up again the next fall, teaching full time with two courses added in English literature, another faculty member met me on campus with saddened eyes. "Haven't you gone back to the kitchen yet?" he asked. "It's getting to be a long war."

One professor, at least, had the civility of Sir Walter Raleigh. When he passed me in the hall on our way to class, he bowed and said, "Good morning, colleague."

With no taste for departmental politics or sitting on committees, I was harmless enough save in the classroom. What ought to have worried them was whether I could talk about Chaucer, Shakespeare, John Milton, and John Donne all in one term without losing my head. There the students helped to quell the vanity and subdue the encircling ego. They would take down your consequence in no time.

They liked to march up just before we began reading *Paradise Lost* and, looking me straight in the eye, say coolly, "I hate Milton." I might have asked, as a professor at Columbia posed the question, "To what deficiency in yourself do you attribute this hostile feeling?" Instead I smiled in sympathy, cursing them under my breath, swearing to myself, "Damn you, that's the last time you'll say that."

Or a girl sent me the season's greetings on a Christmas card: "I am the one who yawned unintentionally while you were speaking of God."

I spoke of God as part of the course, of love oftener still. They were the material, the inevitable themes, of English poetry—heaven and hell, good and evil, love and hate, body and soul, vice and versa.

(Life is a contest between vice and versa, a student wrote, in which versa usually triumphs.)

For classroom study, the subject of love pleased them most, as it pleased me, whether in Eden, in Verona, or in John Donne's bed. They only hoped such pleasures and catastrophes weren't archaic by now or altogether obsolete. Yet one of my colleagues remarked from the rostrum: "It embarrasses me to speak the word *love* out loud." Brave scholar, to teach the language of Shakespeare and Donne and avoid the word, delighting nobody but Donne himself ("For Godsake hold your tongue, and let me love").

In the Shakespeare Concordance are eleven pages with double columns of reference to *love,* after which come *loved, lover, loving,* and *loving-jealous.* Like Shakespeare, who disposed of *hate* with its limited appeal in two columns, the students believed honestly in love, its persistent and reliable nature, for themselves and for the human race. Beyond that Hotspur's courage moved them. Lear's plight was their own.

In the end, though, the popular characters were the clowns—Falstaff, Dogberry, the Wife of Bath—the rascals, the rogues, and the pious wantons. Someone shouting in high spirits, someone fat, foolish, and turbulent, comical as sin, that was little enough to ask of poetry.

"I am a peppercorn, a brewer's horse," they read laughing.

"Write me down an ass!"

"Blessed be God that I have wedded fyve!"

You might say that next to the study of love, lust, longing, dalliance, and desire, they chose laughter holding both its sides. And so did I. And so does any man.

But Professor Irving may have been right. One day he stopped at our table while B. and I were having lunch in the Oak Room. He prepared to sit down with us at the empty place.

"You two seem to be regaling yourselves," he said. "What's the big joke? What are you talking about?"

"Beauty and Truth," I said. "The problem of good and evil and the struggle for men's souls."

"I was explaining to her the age-old conflict of the flesh and the spirit," said B., grinning. "Care to join us?"

"Oh, no!" cried the professor, backing away. "Nobody ever speaks of such things outside the classroom."

III

>>>>>>>>>>>>>>>>>><<<<<<<<<<<<<<<<

To lead a double life is probably a good idea for a woman. She seems created for it, not through the duplicity in her nature—"a woman's a two-face"—or through being (like a man) double in herself as body and soul, but merely by the accident of being female.

"Women are a sex by themselves, so to speak," said Max Beerbohm.

"Women are born to thraldom and penance
And to been under mannes governance," said Chaucer.

"Let Greeks be Greeks, and women what they are,
Men have precedency and still excell," said Anne Bradstreet.

"Most women are croquettes," said one of my students. But that is beside the point.

I wasn't content to be a housewife, though I loved keeping house. The role itself could hardly be nobler: "She was a neate good Huswife every inch," wrote the Puritan poet Edward Taylor of his wife. No praise is higher than that. But I wasn't busy enough rearing children and wiping their noses, doing the housework, making my clothes, washing, ironing, marketing, cooking, mending, gardening, telephoning the plumber, and entertaining friends. The thraldom was lovely under a man's will, but not a whole existence, not a lifelong pursuit. One needed a hobby, a variation of days. Also, a way to justify taking up space on this earth.

We used to call it the Mrs. Roosevelt complex—the urge to rush out and mill around twenty-four hours by the clock fulfilling oneself in the marketplace. My energetic mother, though obliged to work to support herself, had such a complex or syndrome, excess of vitality or surplus of energy. She called it keeping heart and hands full, and she passed it along to me.

Montaigne not only defined the "double man" but lived a delightfully double life by retiring to a tower each morning to get away from his wife, read his thousand books, probe his nature, write his essays, and prosper—safe from frustration and the brevity of his years. He lived, says his biographer Donald Frame, with "scandalous serenity," and died so too. (Yet Sainte-Beuve said of Montaigne, "He lived in an age which a man who had passed through the Terror could call the most tragic age of all history." So we compete for the honor of living in the worst of all possible times.) His words *"Je ne fais rien sans gayeté"* made an honest boast, humbly put. Of course, Montaigne was wiser than to try to teach others—at least in a schoolroom—considering himself too ill-taught, with no authority that would cause men to believe him. I do not teach, he said, I tell. He was content with self-knowledge, modest man.

But I was speaking of the plight of being a woman, not a philosopher (which confuses the issue but has to be borne in mind), and of possible shifts to make the best of it.

Halfway between Mrs. Roosevelt's on the one hand and Montaigne's on the other, my solution was to live three lives: the domestic, the professional, and in an (insubstantial) tower the private. A watchtower, that is, not an ivory. Now after a quarter of a century, fully aware of the vanity and overweening of tripling oneself in a multiple choice of existence, I can highly recommend it to anybody who wants it. The only rule is to remember it won't work, not with scandalous serenity. Each separate life constantly demands its rights in the matter. Each self cries out, "Pity me."

Since Duke with its medieval towers clung to the antediluvian system of holding classes six days a week, I soon asked for a three-day schedule and, with reluctance, by special courtesy of Dean Wannamaker, was granted it. I would be glad to teach all day on either cycle, I told him, not on both cycles.

"An extraordinary request!" said Dean Wannamaker. "What will you do on Mondays, Wednesdays, and Fridays?"

"Not teach," I said.

Everybody wants to write. With the exception of B. who wrote books but didn't want to ("Writing is a dog's life," said B.), I've met few people in the end who didn't plan some day to get around to serious composition. The urge is innate to put oneself on paper, if not a candid camera shot at least a likeness from an interesting angle. Everybody believes he has something in him to say and doubtless has, however quick the critics are to complain that the book inside every man would be better off to stay there. What about a whole bookshelf?

Stored in his head is the material of experience, real as the next person's. A single day in one ordinary woman's life (*Mrs. Dalloway*) or in one man's (*Ulysses*) becomes a tale lucidly drawn, overwhelmingly true, if Virginia Woolf or James Joyce depicts it. The trouble is, writing asks too much: it takes one's life and one's blood, yet who has enough to spare? It takes words. It takes walking naked, and in the end a man may prefer to keep his pants on.

There is, I think, more enterprise in walking naked, though few save the unabashed believe this and they may be right. Ours is still a fig-leaf morality. For most occasions we have reticences to wear, a hero mask or two, a bead for raiment, a crown like Lear. Shakespeare made Lear old and mad before he saw himself stark as unaccommodated man, only a poor, bare, forked animal.

The naked figure stands revealed in the altogether, in body and in mind, exposing himself and his whereabouts. He is clothed, as Rabelais said, in "nothing before, nothing behind, and sleeves of the same"—an enterprise better left, perhaps, to a porcelain figurine or to Renoir's plump bathing nudes or Botticelli's Venus.

In 1942 when we moved to North Carolina, I sat silent in the car during the trip and worried all day about my writing. How soon must I give it up? For the last five years in New York I had kept churning out verses that by now filled a thick black notebook, stirred by some hungry ambition to write them by the thousand, each verse rewritten a thousand times to get the hang of it. So far I had read better rhymes than these. Yet not a line had been rejected by an editor since no editor had been given the chance. As unpublished words they justified themselves, if at all, by existing.

Keats knew he would write though every word were to be destroyed next day, "even if my night's labours should be burnt every morning and no eye ever shine upon them." But he was Keats. It might also be said there were other things in life. Writing for pleasure could be self-delusion, flight from reality—as B. had so often told me—only a childish scribble. No Muse was really saying, "Fool! look in thy heart and write." The Fool was the fool of the farce.

Not in the heart but in the mirror, there let the amateur look. Hope carried one too far. The whole venture was immodest, an acute case of *hubris,* and I wished I was prettier. So I gave myself a year of grace. After such indulgence I would swear off, finish my thesis for the doctor's degree. I braced myself to admit I had nothing to say and had said it badly; meddling with verse was bad. A rhymer. All cry and no wool (like a clipped and shorn sow). No pith.

Despite the stern resolve, three years passed while I put off the act of renunciation and delayed burning my manuscript in the fireplace. There were (the excuse was) too many notable items in North Carolina—Judas trees and January jasmine, Dukes and cardinals, professors and errant college girls, a small Negro boy at Hallowe'en in a chalk white falseface, Lord Cornwallis in a Carolina spring. The tidiness of verse led me on, the vexation of verse.

Besides, I liked to write. It was a pleasure like drawing breath or making love. You could always find the justifiers to defend the crime—Sir Philip Sidney, "It is better to write than lie and groan"; Cummings in his *nonlectures:* "who am I" is answered by "what I write."

Virginia Woolf called it "scrutiny of blank paper." T. S. Eliot called it "turning blood to ink." Aubrey Beardsley put a blot on paper and pushed it around till something happened. The Chinese poet Po Chü-i, a thousand years ago in the ninth century, was a particularly honest justifier:

> There is no one among men that has not a special failing;
> And my failing consists in writing verse.

Like the Victorian Mrs. Barbauld who wrote bad prose ("An ass is much better adapted than a horse to show off a lady") and bad poetry ("Life! I know not what thou art!"), I was a "miscellaneous" writer. Women often are. Everything they undertake is miscellaneous. The women in my family, of a vigorous sort, had managed to keep their hands busy. To avoid anything like an empty, idle moment of leisure, they had reached for their "fancywork"—knitting, crocheting, tatting, quilting, hemstitching, embroidering—anything done with a needle or hook. My mother went so far as to paint flowers on china and burn designs into wood to make bowls and wastebaskets. Then to a woman they put their work away as too fine for ordinary use, laying it neatly folded into chests or storing it in attics till, when they died, there it was, no longer admired or wanted by their inheritors. It had changed with time, its beauty dimmed, its glory lost. It had gone quietly out of fashion.

Somehow I found the idea comforting of my sturdy forebears, those needlewomen whose blood ran in my veins and invigorated them, endlessly stitching their fancywork as—in Yeats's words for his poems, "stitching and unstitching"—I worked at mine. They refused to be idle. They made something into a pattern, then carefully put the finished piece away.

"And yet there are those," said Don Quixote, "who compose books and toss them out into the world as if they were no more than fritters."

One day in 1945 B. took things into his own hands. He had lived with this unsettling performance long enough; his action was that of a cornered man. He swiped my black notebook, wrapped it in brown paper, and without a word sent it off to Boston to the Houghton Mifflin Poetry Contest. When shortly I discovered the notebook missing, B. said he was having it bound for me at the Seeman Printery.

"What a silly thing to do!" I cried in dismay. "I don't *want* it bound."

"I'm sorry. It was just a gesture, love."

"Damn! You might at least have asked my permission."

"I thought it would look nice in a plain simple binding."

"You know perfectly well how it will look. Like some damned Ph.D. *thesis,* that's what!"

36

As any child could see, mine was an unsuitable entry, wrong even in category. It failed to meet the rules for contestants or pass the requirements for poetry, except one might argue it wasn't actually written in prose. B. entered it anyway, casual as a lunch basket, in competition for the Poetry Fellowship Award. The winner that year was the poet Elizabeth Bishop for her first volume, *North and South,* and the judges' choice was unanimous. (When Elizabeth Bishop was asked about her poetic technique, she said, "It all depends." I liked that.)

On June 5 Ferris Greenslet, editor of Houghton Mifflin, wrote to advise me of the results. From eight hundred contestants, he was happy to announce I'd been named runner-up in a race I didn't know I had entered. If his opening words were bewildering therefore, the rest of the letter grew in clarity and charm. My collection of "literate" light verse hadn't seemed quite the ticket to win the award. But the manuscript had pleased the judges, himself one, and Houghton Mifflin asked permission to publish it as a volume.

I blinked and read on. The second of three judges, Katharine White, an editor of the *New Yorker,* wanted a number of pieces for her magazine. Edward Weeks of the *Atlantic Monthly,* the third judge, made the same request. Mohammed had come to the mouse.

The trick, it appeared, was to have a husband at wit's end. What the mailman brought was the answer to one of my three lives, as well as a new lease on it. Had I known beforehand—but I didn't know and I think it better not to. You can't count on an academy award, instead of a rejection slip, by mail.

A few weeks later the four of us drove to New York, where B. went to teach in the graduate school that summer at Columbia University. Where he had been a student he was now a professor. Though we were returning after three long war years away, New York had kept entire, not yet gutted by bombs. The house we rented on Sedgwick Avenue was in the old Bronx neighborhood; the street signs said, "Hurray, you're home." We walked up and down Fordham Road in our own footsteps, touching the storefronts in loving greeting—the delicatessen, the Chinese laundry, the cigar store. They were in business, still upright.

The world had been hurt, much of it destroyed, in these three years. A maniacal war ground slowly to a halt. One year ago, on D Day, June 6, 1944, our troops had landed on a ninety-mile stretch of the Normandy beaches to take Europe away from Hitler. They landed in captive France, and by August 25 Paris had been liberated, a *free* Paris.

It was too soon to rejoice; the Germans were far from beaten. Buzz bombs threatened daily to wipe out London. Nearly nine bloody months had to pass before we staggered out of it, the beginning of the end (on May 8, V-E Day), when with Hitler's suicide Germany had surrendered. Two days before Hitler's death, Mussolini (whom Churchill called "this whipped jackal") was shot by a firing squad with his mistress Clara Petacci. Less than a month earlier, by a fearful coincidence Franklin Roosevelt had suddenly died of cerebral hemorrhage—he who had named it the War of Survival, a war he didn't survive. As he died the Americans were fighting on Okinawa in what would be the last operation of the Pacific War.

Then the thing happened. On a Monday, July 16, while B. lectured on the peaceful and confident Victorians (as a man must surely do his day's labor whether or not planets threaten to vanish), the first atomic bomb was exploded in the desert near Los Alamos. Nobody knew if it would work, not the scientists themselves who had created this death. It worked too well, from that moment able to seal our doom, sufficient to the need, more merciless than war itself. In a shatterable world forever changed, man, intelligent enough to split the atom and make the bomb, had lacked the greater intelligence not to make it. With this final proof of his ingenuity, now he could destroy mankind.

By such an appalling event of history—the coming of the Atomic Age—one tends to date events of one's own life. On that infamous day, I remember, Philip aged twelve went fishing in the Harlem River beside the 207th Street Bridge a few blocks away. While he sat on a concrete pier next to a couple of other fishermen, dangling his line in the water, the bloated corpse of a drowned man floated up at his feet. It was the first dead man Pip had seen. Yet he was old enough to know you can't run away from a mortal spectacle like that. While the police grappled for the body and fished it out, he stayed to watch and learn the look of death, this death—the terrible sea change, the fleshly disintegration of what, perhaps a week before, had been a man.

After he stumbled home, pale and sick from the sight, all I could think to say was to remind him of the commonplace death is, how certain even ordinary an occurrence, a fact he must be aware of as an avid reader of murder mysteries.

"There's always a corpse or two in them, isn't there?" I said.

"Sure there is."

"Bound to be. You can't have a murder story without a corpse in it."

"No."

"Well, that's what you saw today—a corpse."

It was poor comfort, no comfort. "I know," Pip said, "but I *saw* him. And he was really *dead*."

Three weeks later the A bomb fell on Hiroshima, one bomb from one plane, one second to explode. More than half the city in a blinding white flash ceased to exist, erased, blotted out in the first nuclear attack. The crime in Hiroshima was to be a human being, and a hundred thousand died for it. Three days afterward, Nagasaki was hit by a second atomic bomb more powerful than the first—which, you would think, had made its point. The second made no sense whatever. But President Truman promised more, the obliteration of a country, unless Japan sued for peace. Truman called the bomb a "harnessing of the basic power of the universe," while Pope Pius XII warned it would lead to a "Satanic destruction of the human race." What if the Nazis had harnessed that power instead? They would have conquered the world.

On the night before the tragedy of Hiroshima, B. and I went dancing on the Starlight Roof of the Waldorf-Astoria with Molly and Frederick, two friends from home who were visiting us. For entertainment we stayed out most of the night, dancing till the orchestra stopped, walking the streets of New York in the mild August weather.

I was much too happy to go home to bed, though I don't know the reason. It felt good to be alive. Frederick, walking beside me, accused me of being euphoric, and he made it sound worse than being plastered—not only unseemly but obnoxious. This was no time for felicity. Frederick's mind had turned gloomy this summer, filled with dark foreboding. For one thing he was a scientist. For another, his close friend, J. Robert Oppenheimer, was the director of the group in Los Alamos that had designed and set off the atomic bomb.

"Why in hell are you laughing?" he asked irritably. "Is this your way of celebrating the end of the planet? What is there left to laugh about?"

"It's a binge," I said. "Maybe I'm having my last laugh."

While we sat at home eating scrambled eggs for breakfast,

now that daylight had come, B. switched on the radio for the news. Japan, we heard, was fatally hit. An atomic bomb had been dropped on a city whose name we didn't catch or recognize. With destruction so stupefying, at last the war would have to end.

Frederick wouldn't let us say it that simply. He said: "You mean *this* war, not the next. The most we can stop is *this* war."

"But this is the war to end all wars," B. said. "Or was that World War I?"

"That was just the Great War."

I didn't feel like laughing any longer.

On August 14 at dinnertime, 7:00 P.M., President Truman announced by radio Japan's surrender. One listened more numb than victorious. The bomb was inconceivable, inhuman, but we had used it.

The following morning, Wednesday, I telephoned the office of the *New Yorker*, expecting no answer. It seemed polite to make the gesture, since one of the editors, Gus Lobrano, had asked to see me at 11:00 A.M. With the celebration of V-J Day, he would be taking a holiday like everyone else. Americans were not prepared to delay till Mr. Truman made the date official.

For a wonder he answered the telephone. He was alone in the office, waiting for me.

"You didn't come in on my account?" I said.

"I had plenty of work to do," he said. "You've no idea how peaceful it is, not a solitary soul around."

"It's V-J Day."

"So it is. Come another time if you like, or if you object to being lured to Forty-third Street with a strange man. Anyway, I'll be here, sober and harmless."

"I'd love to come."

It was a queer interview, unreal, wonderfully exclusive, since we appeared to be the only two people left in New York, alone in an empty office building. I had never met an editor before, but I couldn't have made a better start than with Gus Lobrano. Dealing with writers had tested his fiber and brought out the inner valor of the man.

He smiled as he handed me the black notebook I hadn't seen since B. told me it had gone to the binders. It looked scuffed. The editors, he said, had chosen thirty poems and wished to offer me a contract, or first-reading arrangement, whereby I would agree to show them in future everything I wrote.

"I accept," I said like a shot. "Writing for you *is* a compliment."

Mr. Lobrano frowned and shook his head in alarm. "No, no!" he said. "You don't understand. I'm sorry, I haven't made myself clear. We do *not* want you to write for us. Ever. What I meant to say, we do not, *don't,* want you to write for us at all. We aren't interested."

I thought I was going to cry.

"It's fatal," he said. "You must never write for anyone but yourself. I couldn't give more fatherly advice. We want to see what you write, but, for the love of mercy, nothing you have written with us in mind. That's the last thing we want."

I said it was no problem. "I guess I wouldn't know how to begin."

"Don't. There's supposed to be a *New Yorker* manner, one part sophistication, one part whimsy. I hope it's not true. There is no formula, method, style, pose that I know of. Writers who look for one fall on their faces—formula writers. They all sound alike, phony."

He told me what a critic was: a man multiplied by six (three might have to do in an understaffed office). Taken singly, any critic was fallible, a snarl of foibles. His head was full of prepossessions and prejudices. His taste couldn't be trusted any more than his judgment. Therefore, at least three editors would have to read and vote in favor of a piece of mine before it could be accepted. A multitude of three.

"Do you mind?" he asked. He was a shy man with a disarming candor, apologetic in handing me Manhattan Island.

"*Mind?*" I said. "I've never had that many readers before."

"Good. Then let's close the interview and go to lunch. What about the Algonquin?"

"The truth is, the real ambition of my life is to eat at the Algonquin and stare at Dorothy Parker." I looked at my watch. "Maybe we're too late."

"We're too late. It's already V-J Day," he said.

I had no interview with Mr. Weeks of the *Atlantic,* but like Gus Lobrano he gave me excellent fatherly advice. In our correspondence he liked to repeat from time to time a ringing phrase that clearly appealed to him.

"Be blithe," he wrote. And again, "Be blithe!"

It sounded familiar, like Chaucer's amiable Host begging his sober pilgrims to be frolicsome and gay: "Telle us some mery thing. . . . Be blythe." It echoed Herrick, whose motto was to live merrily and trust to good verses. It affirmed Sir Thomas More's faith in *festivitas.* It reflected Montaigne's considered view. Montaigne was an independent man with a view, but he would have agreed unhesitating to this one. "Think only pleasant thoughts," he said and found, I believe, the only way to do so: avoid thinking unpleasant ones.

I too agreed, at least in theory, though sometimes I

wondered. How could a person manage? How could he stay light of heart, always in the mood to frisk and chirrup? Suppose the world turned joyless? It would seem not so much lighthearted as lightheaded nowadays to countenance gaiety in poets, especially for a hellgazer like me. This was not the season to be jolly, not a time for foolery and merrymen. One ought to be blighted, not blithe. A doomcrier. So the Comic Spirit goes out weeping.

However, one editor had said, "Write to please yourself." Another had said, "Try to be cheerful about it." The deal looked fair enough, worth the risk.

"Who, I? I have been merry twice and once ere now."

IV

In the next year we lost David at fifteen, who went off to preparatory school at Exeter in New Hampshire. From that time he came home only for holidays, bewilderingly older with each visit, a world away, no longer a tenant of the house. It was too soon to lose him, a sundering, the more so since (from reading Thomas Wolfe) I was convinced you can't go home again. Now I know better. Nothing is more untrue. I know you go back over and over again, seeking the self you left behind. Thomas Wolfe made a career of looking homeward to tell his story.

At Exeter, David wrote, he was singing "second base" in the Episcopal choir, running cross-country track, and taking long walks to look at the white pines of New Hampshire "and other gymnosperms." Often his letters sounded lonely, and I wondered what on earth we were thinking of to deprive him of girls and high-school dances and the chance to become an Eagle Scout.

Then his English instructor, Darcy Curwen, whom we hadn't met, wrote to explain how it was with David: "I don't know any boy in school who savors so completely and lives so vividly every second as Dave does. He really is all right." After that everything was all right. But it was too soon to lose him.

We lost at the same time the little white house on Nation Avenue, with its beautiful telepathic trees and extrasensory perception, when the Pratts who owned it returned after Mr. Pratt's period of war service. The housing shortage had become so acute we were banished and homeless. We had nowhere to go.

With the Pratts due to materialize like ectoplasm on the doorstep (he was a parapsychologist too), we drove up and down the countryside in a forlorn search for an empty farmhouse or, after a while, even a sharecropper's cabin or a small Baptist church in a pine grove. We begged a roof over our heads in the neighboring towns of Hillsborough and Chapel Hill, to no avail. No refuge was left, nothing but a room in the Washington Duke Hotel.

"At eleven dollars a day?" B. asked.

"We'll go straight to Dean Wannamaker," I said. "We'll do this: walk in, resign our jobs, and walk out. If Duke University won't lift a finger to keep us, it can charge ahead without us. We'll go back to New York where we belong."

"And stay the winter at the Waldorf," B. said. "There's nowhere to live in New York either, you know that. We couldn't find an apartment to rent. We couldn't get a room in a flophouse for the night."

I wanted to go away, return to my own latitudes. I had had enough of the South, a bellyful of Dixie. It made me feel unwelcome, like an uncongenial guest, an outsider graciously endured during his brief sojourn but not for a moment accepted as belonging. It wasn't my element at all. I was a damnyankee among a lot of damned Tar Heels.

Then B. bought us a house at a cocktail party.

He bought it from Charles Ward, a professor in our department, who was about to go on sabbatical leave for the year and, besides, found living six miles in the country not to his liking. The cocktail party was in full blast, a faculty romp louder by the minute, when B. heard a rumor of the Ward house being possibly for sale. Sprinting through the crowd till he found Charles, B. took a death grip on him, shouted in his ear an offer to buy at any price and pay cash on the spot, then began a rapid search through his pockets. Charles's wife, standing near, shook her head to warn her husband B. had had one martini too many.

"Do you keep that much cash on you?" she asked innocently.

"My God, no, nor anywhere else," B. said, his hands trembling. "I was only looking for a cigarette."

It was a white brick house, perched solid as a cloud on a low hill set about with triangular cedars and loblolly pine. Surrounding were two acres of lawn and the rest pine woods —a greensward and a greenwood—five acres in all plus a meadowful of Mr. Easley's cows. The enormous paneled living room was arranged (as four walls ought to be) for a piano at one end, books at the other, little else between but windows and a fireplace—a room to anchor to. It stood one story high with two tall chimneys on the Guess Road beyond the Eno River. If you cared to guess where Guess Road went, it went nowhere.

This is the very house where I live today in a countryside that is mine, I hope, for as long as forever is. Its landscape is the landscape of my mind. "My attachments are all local," said Charles Lamb.

As if on first acquaintance, we came in touch with the seasons and found them excellent company. The seasons in North Carolina were always slightly askew; the calendar stayed Gregorian but the year tended to get ahead of itself. Our sap rose early down here, before the sap in Massachusetts. Nobody knew what time it was. The Mayflies mated in

April, the June bugs buzzed in May, the January jasmine bloomed in December. We had meadow violets and fireworks for Christmas. Confederate violets, that is.

A good year might start off with spring and end with fall, skipping to winterspring except for a spell of blackberry winter in May when the blackberry blossomed. Or we might have hominy snow in tiny balls on the crimson japonica in early April. Madame de Sévigné said she felt capable of making, if need be, a spring herself. Personally I never needed to. There was more spring around here than one knew what to do with.

We heard some peculiar birdsong. In June the whippoor-will sounded through the night, dull and throbbing like a pulse beat, an African tom-tom (*"Tom-tom, c'est moi"*), harping on nothingness. (John Burroughs counted 1,478 whippoorwill calls before falling into exhausted sleep, but he didn't have insomnia like me.) When the bird left off by the light of day, the mockingbird picked up the refrain, slightly off-key as if he'd been at it all hours or had a screw loose, a great cheat pretending to be a whippoorwill. It was like the old-style country music of the South, twangy and monotonous:

> Who is this fool, astandin here,
> Athinkin he is me?

Even sitting on the ridgepole, the mockingbird passed itself off as a windsock or TV aerial. Amorist in May, it sang the night through in a nonstop songflight noisy as a guitar, trilling borrowed notes of joy in imitation of the cardinal— who began his own morning song, "Cheer, cheer, cheer," promptly at 4:10 A.M. Three cheers, he cried, for the official bird of the State of North Carolina. In this racket the only thing a bird didn't do was sing like William Cullen Bryant, "Spink, spank, spink."

Everywhere were the revelations. One December a gray

fox visited our wood. One summer a white heron five feet tall came and stood pensive on one leg under the weeping willow, looking expectant like a stork. I think he did it on purpose, eyeing me, making me understandably anxious.

Everywhere were the lessons: the language to learn, the essence of the place, the simplicities. ("I was determined to know beans," said Thoreau at Walden.) I learned when pigs are in clover their pigtails whirl completely around in ecstatic spirals. A fairy ring is made of mushrooms. Ladybugs are sometimes male (about half of them are. How humiliating).

"What kind of bug is that?" asked a man.

"Why, that's a ladybug."

"Say!" said the man, "you've got good eyes."

I learned the name of things, to tell a hawk from a heron, a fact from a fancy. The black hellebore in the garden, sprung from Hades ("Some live on hellebore and some on hope"), whose other name was Christmas rose, was no rose to me. It was sinister, unChristian, kin to hemlock and nightshade, deadly as a mandrake that shrieks and drips blood. Beside the hellebore I planted bleeding hearts. A light rain was called bird sweat, a sprinkle was a shirttail shower, a heavy rain a frog-strangler. The tiny flower with the pansy face growing on the terrace, that was heartsease. To my surprise I had a lot of singing titmice.

Howard Easley taught me country matters: how, say, to tell a steer from a bull. In passing his barn I called out praise of his handsome bull.

"Steer, dearie," Howard said.

"He's sticking his head out of the stable window," I said. "How can I tell a steer by his horns?"

"The same way you tell a male tree from a female tree," Howard said. "By looking between the limbs."

"So skeptics are gone to milk the bull," I said. I learned that from Dr. Johnson.

From time to time Howard changed drastically the meadow

scene—from a ceremony of grazing Herefords, lined up and moving abreast like chorus girls, to a flowering mead of red clover; from red clover to a cornfield rippling in the wind, shining in the rain, gleaming in the sun with gold tassels. No matter what occupied the place, the fence round it was "pig tight, bull strong, and stud-horse high," which made me feel safer than Europa when the one real bull among the heifers wandered up to look me over with a speculative eye. He was less a Zeus than a Ferdinand.

At breakfast of a spring morning we watched Howard riding wildly around the ploughed field on his tractor, driving with one hand and making outflung gestures with the other, his head thrown back like a man with a message, waving his left arm in eloquent, wide-sweeping arcs.

"What the devil is he throwing about?" I asked B.

"Benisons," he said.

In March Mr. White of Selborne sowed leeks and larkspurs. Howard sowed benisons.

The funny thing was that he loved to farm as I loved to write. A Duke professor who had retired from teaching after two heart attacks, he lusted for the repetition of days, ploughing the same old meadow, sowing, reaping, ploughing again. Or letting in the cows. He didn't make a living at it, and the cows were hardly grateful. He kept busy, "windblown and out of breath" he called it, moving with the seasons. The only difference between us was that Howard might have to give up when it rained. I would sit at my typewriter on the porch and think how much we were alike in our work —my friend and brother Sisyphus. *Mon semblable, mon frère.*

One day I put a piece of paper in the typewriter and wrote: "Beulah was murdered yesterday." The words looked improbable, as they had when I read them in the paper that morning. The man with whom she was living, Clifton Jones, enraged that she had run him out of the house, sawed off a shotgun, hid it under his coat, and came back to kill her.

My mind was overfull of Beulah, "Sometime" Beulah, who worked for me five or six years in this countryside and came either when she said she would or sometime. With six small children she had borne a year apart—breast child, lap child, knee child, yard young'un—she didn't always make it, but my heart rejoiced when she hove in sight, black, neat, and beautiful, walking slowly through the meadow up from her house. Often she brought the six children along, dressed and polished as for Sunday school, and they sat decorous as blackberries in a solid row on the terrace while she worked. "I'd sooner live under a lone pine tree," she told me, "than go off and leave my children needing my love."

The night the seven children disappeared (her own six plus a young niece), Beulah with Willie, her husband, came straight to us, and we left our beds to call the sheriff. At two o'clock on Sunday morning, Beulah and Willie, just returned from a night in town, smelled strongly of wine. Willie wept. "My poor children, drowned in the Eno," he sobbed. But Beulah was calm, like the sheriff and his assistant, who squatted on our doorstep and looked up at the summer sky.

We talked from time to time, as the night passed, about the possible whereabouts of seven lost children. Only Willie provided a clue. "Drowned in the Eno, all dead, dead in the Eno," he told us through his tears. The sheriff shook his head, explaining that while one child might fall into the river and drown itself, you'd never in your life find seven drowning at one swoosh.

"And he's the one to know," said Beulah.

He seemed curiously unwilling to begin scouring the countryside, even to be concerned. It was a Southern moonlight night, too hot for action, and the sheriff sat back on his heels to do his figuring. Finally he beckoned B. to follow him into the house, where he revealed how simple things looked to him.

"Beulah there," said the sheriff. "I know her family of old. They have themselves a mess of trouble."

"But this *is* trouble!" B. exploded. "Seven children, vanished into thin air, one of them a small infant. God knows where they are."

"That's purely true."

"And it's the middle of the night!"

"They'll turn up," said the sheriff. "It's not but three o'clock."

At 4:00 A.M. they turned up with no help from the law. Philip found them. All at once he jumped to his feet and ran across the lawn to the house next door, whose owners were away. There he found the seven children huddled together on the floor of the back porch, fast asleep. They were afraid to stay home alone, they said, after Philip wakened them and led them to our house. They had run away lugging the baby to look for a hiding place.

Our last view that night was of Beulah, striding through the field behind the long line of wailing children, cuffing them at each step, loudly threatening them with more blows. "Don't whip 'em, Beulah," Willie moaned, bringing up the rear. "Don't whip 'em, Beulah."

Beulah and Willie left our countryside and moved to the other end of town. The last I heard, until this morning, was a rumor of Beulah having walked out one day and abandoned Willie. What became of the six children, from the baby Isaiah to the sweet-faced Skip, I never knew. Someone said she had gone to live with a man named Jones.

The twelve months in North Carolina ran their course more or less dependably like this:

JANUARY. Perhaps a single white crocus. If you had enough crocuses—interwoven lavender, white and gold—you had a Persian rug. A bee was in the hellebore, making poison honey. According to the Greeks, hellebore mixed with honey would kill mice.

In the first warm sun, out rushed the camellias, foolish delicate white flowers. They sallied out like young virgins and were soon nipped. Camellias never learn, innocent as the blessed damozel.

I said, "Somewhat eats the crocus in the garden" (Mr. White of Selborne wrote in his *Journal*, "Somewhat eats the pinks," and thirteen days later added "Hares").

The neighbors gathered to supply the answer, which was varied but authoritative. My neighbors held plenty of convictions. One said rabbits. One said moles. One said, "It's those doggone blackbirds!" A fourth declared, "Wood rats. My wife thinks field mice, but I say no, wood rats."

"Cut worms," I said. By now I could afford to be as wrong as the next man, free to air an opinion. My honest opinion was that somewhat ate the crocus.

FEBRUARY. The peepers tuned up, stirring the mild night air to announce it was time to make love, like the radio commercial, "It's time, it's time, it's time to fertilize." A spring opera. A madrigal of dillydally. Pipe and drum music for field and stream. Spring was traveling north from Miami at the rate of seventeen miles a day, climbing mountains, fording rivers, to wake the one-inch male peepfrogs to enchant the females with anticipatory song.

The breath of spring was sweet. It was a flowering bush.

Once in February a field mouse ran across B.'s face in the night and woke him. "I won't tell Helen," he said to himself and slept again. But in the morning signs of mice were in the kitchen. Sometimes they dropped in for warmth and charity.

"Why would a mouse pick a human being to creep over?" I asked.

"He didn't know it was a human being, love," B. said. "He thought it was just another mouse."

MARCH. The weeping willow came out in light-green tears. Marvell found nothing so amorous as green. The rest was regal with heraldic colors: the *jaune* and *purpure* of daffodils and hyacinths.

I had a weeping tree, an umbrella tree, a silktree, a Judas tree, a rooftree, but no philosopher's tree.

Athenaeus told of a philosopher who watered the lettuce in his garden with wine and honey. Mr. Jefferson of Monticello advertised in Europe for a gardener who could play the French horn.

Willie chased a calf two *hours* old around the meadow, trying to catch it, while its mother bawled at her child in helpless wonderment. I asked, "How long does it take before a calf will stand and suck?"

He replied, "This one hardly hit the ground."

APRIL. There was the splash of scarlet azaleas. And dogwood, dogwood, dogwood, like a light-fallen snow in the woods. We owned five acres of April. A barometer on the porch read Fair on clear days and Fair on foul, with gusts of rain wetting its face. Like Thoreau, it failed to record bad news.

A fleeting honor was to be a waystation for migrant birds. Yellow finches flying north joined the dandelions on the lawn, covering it with solid gold blur. Next day only dandelions.

The Age of Jet, when it came, was marked by an eerie white streak zigzagging the sky. At sunrise you were roared from your bed by a booming chariot of dawn—Aurora on her silver wheels drawn by white-winged horses kicking up a rosy cloud behind them.

A scientist at Duke reported on the memory of earthworms. When an earthworm was cut in two and each half tested separately, the front end exhibited more memory than the back end.

In the spring term while we read Keats's "Isabella; or The Pot of Basil," I brought to class a garden pot of basil, green and thriving, that the students might imagine Lorenzo's severed, moldering head buried in it by Isabella, wet by her tears, with Lorenzo "vile with green and livid spot" richly feeding the plant. This is known as a teaching device.

MAY.   March will search and April try,
         May will tell you if you'll live or die.

Whoever gathered nuts in May? For answer I consulted Brewer's Dictionary, which said: " 'Here we go gathering nuts in May.' *See* Nuts."

At 6:00 P.M. Howard telephoned: "I drove to your house to bring you fresh strawberries for dinner, but I saw by your pattern of lights you were getting ready to go out. So I went back home." The words gave me a safe, neighborly feeling all evening. "The pattern of lights," I thought.

Horace Walpole hated that "unpleasant Christian commodity, neighbors."

As we came up our spiral driveway at night, the headlights would pick out a cottontail hightailing it ahead. The white button was all you saw, the tail end of Peter Rabbit, who mistook us for the great horned owl hot in pursuit. Marianne Moore said she wondered why rabbits have long ears (facts made Marianne Moore "profoundly grateful"). But she never came wondering up my driveway.

Chekhov, in a letter dated May: "There is the smell of grass." And the voice of the mourning dove.

JUNE. A bevy of nine little quail walked in the dooryard, farther off a murmuration of meadowlarks. Bluebirds on the wing were like aquamarines. But no greater or lesser yellowlegs—they frequented the Carolina coast. No swans or peacocks. No popinjay within these precincts.

A lady birdwatcher came and stood in the woods to listen. "That's the most exotic bird I've ever heard," she said. "What is it, I wonder?"

"A squirrel."

Neighbor John passed through the yard with Betsy, his pointer, in heat. Out in front long-legged Betsy loped along straining at the leash, then John moving at top speed switch in hand, followed by a hard-breathing procession of curs— the mongrel Zip, next a little feist twelve inches high, and a large assortment of beagles yipping loudly. The panting admirers kept in strict line, with John flourishing the whip—a man walking a dog the hard way, for Betsy a moment of puffery. It could have been worse. Up the road apiece lived the Fergusons with twenty-three English cocker spaniels.

JULY. Chiggers in the grass, cicadas afiddle in the trees, the summer replacement of brown thrashers (the color of wholewheat bread) for mockingbirds, and red tanagers for cardinals kindling the trees. Our neighbors the Koches had a scarlet Alfa Romeo. We had redbirds.

The twenty gardenias on the Sears,Roebuck gardenia bush bloomed into Chanel No. 5, so that in the night I dreamed a smell and smelled a dream. Catullus wrote his friend Fabullus of an overpowering sweet ointment: "When you have had one whiff of it, you will beg the gods to make you all nose."

Days were like festivals when everybody ate Mr. Easley's corn: friends and neighbors, faculty and administration, plus farmers, hunters, townspeople, county commissioners, well diggers, bystanders, lookers-on and passersby, plus workmen and Negro help, plus pigs, cows, field mice, corn borers, and the two riding horses. It was free.

Howard grew sweet corn to give away not, he said, out of beneficence but to protect himself against the weather and the eye of the Lord, both of which would break your heart. I felt the same way about writing for a living. The cost in worry was too high, the likelihood of starving to death too fretful and certain a thing.

One day Cornelia (who helped me after Beulah left) and I went down to Howard's lower field to pick some corn. The earth was muddy after rains and, absorbed in finding my way, I all but stepped on a thick snake about three feet long. It and I moved fast in opposite directions. Cornelia ran like a fleet deer. Then she stopped and laughed. "Oh, laws, it's nothing in the world but an old black snake!" As we picked the corn she said, "The next thing we'll see is a *bear*."

"No, Cornelia," I said. "No bears!" But I looked beyond at the acres of cornfield framed by woods. A lonely place.

"My husband saw one before he died," she said. "You never know."

AUGUST. Apricot-colored days in the inextinguishable lemon sun, a topaz summer, amber and gold. (Van Gogh: "How lovely yellow is!") At night a halo on the moon for rural electrification.

B. complained that all the money in the house went for typewriter ribbons, admitting they cost less than hamburgers at the beach. Black ribbons and white paper gave a pleasure like sand and wind and sea.

"August is the mute month," wrote Mr. White of Selborne. The hoopla was over. August slept. The only country sounds came from the rattle of my typewriter, the tick, tick of grasshopper words in my head, Wallace Stevens whispering in my ear: "Of what is this house composed if not of the sun?" "What is there in life except one's ideas, Good air, good friend, what is there in life?"

The freedom to go nowhere. The summer of a dormouse.

SEPTEMBER. A green lizard appeared on the dot as the hummingbird had in June, each three inches long, each peering in through the porch screen. The hummingbird had flown perhaps five hundred miles across the Gulf of Mexico in a single night, brave enough to fight eagles. Where had this green snoop come from? It flattened its lithe body and tapering tail and held on, unblinking, regarding me with no wild surmise. "You're back," I said.

According to Howard, the three things no woman could do, at least in his presence, were: play poker ("Why skin a flea for its hide and tallow?"), hunt possum, or attend his September beer party.

A cricket sang on the hearth to recordings of Bach and Handel.

September hurricanes moved up the coast at eight or ten miles an hour, faster than spring but less welcome. While we heard by radio of 150-mile ill winds at Key West, the sun shone on the marigolds, not a leaf-rustle stirred the trees. Our turn hadn't come to greet the laggard killer. No need to quake for a day or two.

OCTOBER. Chrysanthemums took over in the garden. We were in another gold, or fool's gold, phase, with showers of yellow leaves falling in the sunlight. Ben Jonson asked:

> What need hath nature
> Of silver dishes, or gold chamber pots?

A magnificat of bickering birds—jays and mockingbirds, screaming, cawing, jeering, mocking, cursing like a flock of black crows—this we called branch song. Prick song or snatches. Frenzy music.

In the column "Around the Garden" in the New York *Times,* the fall slogan was: "How wonderful to be a seed at this time of year! What travels!" How carefree to whiffle about on a puff of wind. But I don't know. I asked myself: which would you rather be—a man or a milkweed?

NOVEMBER. Swept in by a single yellow butterfly. Yet the buzzards sailed round like monstrous swooping bats overhead, insolent and silent, a black circling shadow of death with a red crown. It was the month, said Bishop Warburton, when little witches drowned themselves and big witches sold themselves to the devil.

"The bloom is gone, and with the bloom go I."

I gathered gold maple leaves for Howard to grind up as mulch for his wife's orchids. Howard gave away his turkeys. I gave him golden leaves, not a bad return.

DECEMBER. Our countryside had a prison farm down the road beyond the Eno River. While I typed at my desk, the shadow of a man would appear at the window inches away, gaping in at me. "Just a convict," I told myself, smiled and nodded, and went on working. He was there to draw water from the outside tap for the prison gang working on the road—murderers, rapists, wife deserters, child beaters, arsonists, burglars, thieves. The early pioneers had only Indians; we had convicts. One came to think of them as neighbors.

So the drama unfolded: a yardful of starlings and the mistletoe trees—huge clumps of mistletoe inaccessible for kissing under as eagles' nests at the top of the black gum tree. All we needed was a mistletoe picker; and a missel thrush to eat the missel berries.

Howard was busy distributing holly by the cartload. I longed to call him Father Christmas because of his professed contempt for this season of dutiful giving. But he would have replied with one of his gentler reproofs, "Keep it clean, dearie." Or, if I persisted, "You're a frog-eyed liar and your feet aren't mates."

I freely admit it wasn't only honeysuckle and morning-glories (both of them pests, anyway, in the South). It didn't always put one in mind of nirvana, or of Vermeer's Delft with its undisturbed moments of placidity. The serenity was not absolute. The peace did not pass understanding. The world was quiet and the house was calm, sometimes.

Now and again a spell of catastrophe or folly darkened the sky, as it will, and thunderpeal rocked the countryside. The apple trees were attacked by scale and the codlin moth. An occasional well went dry. A neighbor died or moved away. Eleanor, Howard's wife, was bitten one day by a copperhead. She put her hand into a mass of wildflowers by the side of the road, and the snake lifted its head and took her by the thumb. Howard rushed her and the snake together to the hospital, though of the two only Eleanor survived. The pain of the bite was excruciating but, being herself a doctor, she had acted quickly and was soon out of danger.

Then I too went out to meet mischance by lifting some stones down in the woods, where I managed to pick up inside my blouse a black widow spider. After sitting idle awhile on the porch gazing at the sunset, I wandered into the house to take a shower and while undressing found the big shiny baleful thing. She hadn't grown angry enough to attack and perhaps kill me. She gave me a reprieve. Yet for days I kept thinking of Robert Lowell's poem that ends, "This is the Black Widow, death."

Afterward I happened to tell a Yankee friend about these mild Carolinas, how we lived in a temperate paradise, *le meilleur des mondes possibles,* with no more than six menaces to life, limb, and the pursuit of survival—copperheads, black widow spiders, ticks, chiggers, termites, and hurricanes (not to count the poison ivy and an occasional tornado).

"What about people?" he asked.

V

>>>>>>>>>>>>>>>><<<<<<<<<<<<<<<<

Over the years I taught various courses at Duke and both sexes. A so-called "Creative Writing" course was in some ways the happiest I ever had. After a year of it, when Newman asked me to continue next fall with a new batch of young writers, I said prayerfully, *"Please,* never again!"

"Why not?" he asked.

"I don't know how."

We met in the late afternoon, a dozen of us around a table as they read their stories aloud—talking, arguing, laughing, and drinking tea. Ants got in the sugar. We became as friendly as Alcoholics Anonymous. I could think of no better arrangement short of placing one teacher and one student at either end of a log.

I urged them to heed F. L. Lucas on Style (in general they did not) : "It is bad manners to give readers needless trouble. Therefore clarity. It is bad manners to waste their time. Therefore brevity." To be brief and clear at the same time was asking the perfection of Giotto's O. I resolved to be lenient.

I told them to set down whatever they liked, but preferably to draw it from their own backyard and make it visible. In general they did. Writing is a personal thing, I said (as if

I knew what it is). Be an authority on yourself; write to please yourself. Tell what is true, it being more entertaining and a lot more plausible than the untrue. Keep a notebook (oh, I told them). A writer is first and last a notetaker or he isn't a writer. Collect places and people instead of inventing them. Why imagine an incident if you have a reliable memory of one? The knack is to find a way of looking, a talent for experience.

All I knew was this, it wasn't easy, words being obdurate. Archibald MacLeish said, "You have to have a writer who can write before you can teach him how"—an adorable answer. You can't give him anything unless he possesses it already.

Of the eight men in the class, two had just returned to college after three or four years as G.I.s in World War II. To them a campus was unreal. They were veterans, not students. They felt self-conscious and awkward trying to be undergraduates again. As for a way of looking at experience, one of them had fought at Iwo Jima.

He was a Marine in the assault force that took the tiny island (the toughest of the Pacific islands to take) after thirty-six days of terrific fighting, much of it man-to-man killing with the Japanese. He had that story to tell. Obsessed by it, reliving the horror, he set himself to describe the battle of Iwo Jima that ended in a final mopping up on March 26, 1945, with him guilty of being alive. Nearly five thousand Americans were killed, but he lived, not even wounded. The scars were all interior.

The words never came. He couldn't dredge them up to say what had happened, nor so much as give a picture of the volcanic island of less than eight square miles. The novelist John Marquand, who watched some of the fighting from the bridge of the *Nevada,* wrote that the place had the "faint delicate colors of a painting on a scroll of silk." My student couldn't report how it looked from a nearer view. He would close his eyes and clench his hands, seeing the beaches, foxholes, shattered pillboxes, piled-up corpses, the raising of the flag that February day when they took Mt. Suribachi. In my office to talk it over, he dropped his head in despair. This he needed to get down on paper and forget—the sound of mortar fire, the step-by-step advance through shell craters, the ferocious smell of blood and death. He called his unwritten story "Fear."

I wanted to make sense, teach without hypocrisy or rectitude. But what did I in this cloistered world insulated from war know of Iwo Jima? Nobody could say it for him. Nobody could tell him how.

"What did you wear?" I asked once.

"*Wear?*" (God, only a woman would ask that.) "Well, you know, my combat gear, helmet, uniform, gun with bayonet—what any private wears. Why would I tell that, for crying out loud?"

I don't know why. The Greeks at Marathon came running in bronze helmet, breastplate and greaves, bronze shield and sword. They met the turbaned Persians carrying spears and drove them in panic to the sea.

The rest of the class wrote merrily on, suffering no pain. Several have since become successful editors and publishers. Not one so far as I know is a professional writer. My record as teacher was 100 per cent perfect.

I always hoped Colbert would get his novel written about a character named George. Any plot that occurred to him, whether for a short story or a long one, always happened to a hero by the name of George. It struck me as a limitation of passionate experience. Even intimidating. (I knew a basset hound named George.) There must be more to life than that, I said. Eventually you'll come to the end of what George can do, which was poor criticism, since so far George had barely made a start. Still, the choice kept Colbert happy and creative. He had that much that was eternal. He placed his fingers on the typewriter keys, and the story would begin: "George . . ."

Then somebody thought up a diabolic plan to teach the freshmen how to write by an improved method, best described as cheek to cheek, or eye to eye. The instructor faced, out of a class of eighteen, each student alone each week to read her theme with her, after which the student burst into tears. At last the classic trauma—one to teach, one to weep. As an ordeal it was grueling, less for student, who was collapsible, than for instructor, who furnished the Kleenex. I had the honor of naming the course, sometime after a friend of mine, a Harvard professor, inquired, "What are you trying to do down there at Duke, kill off your English faculty?"

We called it the Killer course.

I learned endurance from it and further indisputable proof that my tongue was loose. In the twenty minutes allotted to each girl each week, I read aloud her humbly offered five-hundred-word paper, noted the latest errors in spelling, grammar, punctuation, syntax, and sentence construction, explained why they were errors or at least eccentricities, discussed her outlining, organization, rhetoric, idiom, topic sentence, and use of the paragraph, and looked up several words in the dictionary to show her their common and accepted meaning. (For example: *cowtail*, as in "Sir Lancelot loved Guinevere and cowtailed to her.")

That was a mere beginning. What really mattered, of course, was what she had to say. So we launched into an inquiry of her aims, intentions, omissions, and limitations in dealing with the subject matter, which elicited from her the inaudible story of her life and a choked confession of her present social commitments (she had joined a sorority, she was hopelessly in love) that had kept her from writing her masterpiece.

Last came a moment of reflection and the placing of the grade on the theme, along with a word of praise to soften the blow, which left her desolated, anywhere from crushed to heartbroken. It was like breaking a butterfly. She burst, one girl described it, "into a vale of tears." An occasional A made me weepier than my moist victim, who cried this time for joy. There wasn't a dry eye in the house.

Meanwhile I would be so far behind with appointments that the queue formed outside my office and straggled down the hall like a breadline. Admitting defeat, routed and time-ridden, I bought an alarm clock, which went off like a siren at twenty-minute intervals and scared me into silence and out of whatever I was about to say.

I loved the freshmen dearly, as one loves a docile child who takes all one's time and love. They were like puppies. They swirled and barked around me like the hellhounds of remorse. And my suspicion grew that the tutorial method, teaching by encounter, was wasted on most of them because they didn't care that much how they wrote. The idea faltered. The effect of higher education was at most fitful. When the nymphs were departed, they could always watch television after marriage and, without wincing, hear *like* used as a conjunction. They could dangle their participles and forget thankfully about Style, most of all their own. They could ignore words as objects, the la-di-da of language.

On the other hand, for this student or that a little help or advocacy was of earthshaking importance. It might change the course of her life. I knew. Mine had been changed.

When Henry Adams taught history at Harvard for seven long years, he found of his many educations the one of teacher the thinnest, with himself a failure at teaching. I'll bet he *was* bad. You can't be a wilted begonia and teach. Yet his discovery was shrewd that the number of students with responsive minds added up, in his experience, to no more than one in ten. The other nine minds couldn't be caught. Only the tenth man listened, responded, and in spite of his teacher learned.

I told this story sometimes to a student or a class, ending with the moral, "You see, *you* are that tenth student. Each one of you is. You have to believe that or you're lost." When I was in college I believed it of myself. The professor took pains to teach me because I was teachable, hot for certainties.

A girl (one of the passionate few who cared to know what any word means) related what happened to her one day while walking with a lady dean, who confided the dramatic tale of her love affair many years ago. The tale illustrated, said the dean, it is the little things in life that count. While she and her young man stood on a bridge, gazing down at the stream during a romantic stroll, the young man expectorated into the water. It was too much, a little thing but too much. She returned his ring and broke with him on the spot.

As soon as she decently could, the student excused herself and raced to her room. Bursting open the door, to her roommate's astonishment she dashed to consult the dictionary on her desk. After a moment's search, she closed the book in disgust.

"Oh, ye gods," she said, "it only means spit."

My own course—mine since I invented it and for years delivered it solo (who else would want to?)—was in modern poetry. More accurately, the poetry of the twentieth century. Twenty years back it was considered a bastard course, avant-garde and unholy, scorned and disdained by the full professors. (At U.C.L.A., there is now a Professor of Avant-Garde Studies, author of *The Erotic Revolution.*) This time Newman White had gone too far in letting me teach what I pleased, as some professors indignantly reminded him. The subject was rash, deplorable, and transitory, dealing with living men in the contemporary world, not yet safely part of the history of the durable past. It was without perspective or accumulated wisdom, by nature frivolous. And so was I.

Who could deny the justice of their view when the course was everything they said? They were wise and enlightened scholars. They had reason to be skeptical. Yet ten years later these same unproved poets were being taught all over the place—by fools like me—in freshman and sophomore courses, genre courses, American and English literature, elocution, comparative literature, seminars, tutorials, the graduate school, school of religion, school of education, and department of art and aesthetics. The less the poets were read by an indifferent public, the more expansively they moved into the curriculum.

The other day a graduate student confessed she had studied (she said been exposed to) the poetry of Yeats in *seven* courses at Duke during her undergraduate years.

"What are you reading now in the graduate school?"

"Yeats," she said.

Well, it was some gain. Twenty years ago she would have been deep in the stanzas of John Greenleaf Whittier.

I expected no more than a handful of students to elect my senior course or care a hoot about reading T. S. Eliot or Ezra Pound. "The age is not propitious to poetry," said the New York *Times,* in perfect agreement with the full professors. But the students did choose, and the class had to be limited to forty each term.

Whatever their unpropitious age was up to, they wanted to hear about it. Mr. Eliot, they thought, was the man to tell them. When he told them their world was a wasteland and they were Prufrocks and Sweeneys, non-heroes, hollow men, defeated and loveless, living as damned souls in a hell of boredom and loneliness, it came as no surprise. This was as they had suspected.

"I see myself in the Prufrock poems," they wrote. "I also can see my parents, my boyfriend, and my roommate. All this becomes very personal. It is even similar to the relation between me and my brother (whose birthday is Thursday)."

"We students are hellgazers," they wrote, "steeped in the wasteland tradition, like Prufrock paralyzed to act. There's nothing wrong with being a hellgazer. It is a common habit among young people. But the effect of seeing myself in a mirror is devastating."

They said: "Like Prufrock I too am afraid, not of asking, afraid there really isn't any answer."

And they summed it up: "After reading Eliot, I feel too lousy and depressed to want to do anything but go to bed."

Only one student refused to label himself. "I am not beyond passion but before it," he wrote, not having lived long enough to find life desolate. I was delighted with him, the one rebel, for answering back.

Yet Eliot had made the age-old discovery (like Oedipus, like Lear) that it is hard to be a man. It is harder to be a man than a poet.

Concern for their misbegotten world seemed to my students a valid concern, as it seemed to me. It might prepare us for what came next. As I write now at the start of the 1970's, I wonder if it prepared us. To my dismay I think it did, though my uninformed guess about the future was each year consistently wrong. Tomorrow, I assumed, the world would mend its ways, *tout passe.* By mid-century we would look back astounded, sighing with relief at our hairbreadth escape into a saner life.

The French novelist Romain Gary recently estimated that for the human race the next twenty thousand years will be critical. After that, in less than a thousand generations (if the planet is still here), things may ease up. The cosmologist Fred Hoyle predicted in his book *Encounter with the Future* that the world is in for a cycle of calamities till a new species of man appears with an average I.Q. of 150. He may have sense enough to survive. Bertrand Russell doubted we would last out the twentieth century.

In the late 1940's we glanced ruefully over our shoulders, askance around us. The class in English 134 shook in its boots, at the same time declaring a preference for happier scenes of rejoicing. In world views it favored rosy ones. A lifetime burning in every moment, please. And in the unreadable future, only peace and love. It might well have asked, like Shaw, "Why was I born with such contemporaries?"

I used to imagine compiling a text of available poems (not yet published as a single distressful volume)—a collection of the absolute, terrifying statements of the human predicament, messages of panic like "The Waste Land," some of "The Cantos," George Barker's dirge "Calamiterror," Cecil Day Lewis's "Overtures to Death," W. H. Auden's "Age of Anxiety," and so on. The waiting-for-the-end boys. These would add up to an indictment of the twentieth century, a panorama of chaos and misrule beyond anything man has known, a new age of darkness, a permanent crisis with its timetable of disaster.

We were, it seemed, in big trouble, living our horrified lives in a perpetual nightmare of self-loathing, *angst,* hate, "terror and concupiscence and pride." We were guilty of ourselves, people with death inside them. The Enemy, without and within, included the world, everyone in it, and oneself. Te-tum, te-tum. "The game is up for you and for the others," warned Auden,

> Here am I, here are you:
> But what does it mean? What are we going to do?

Was it then a true picture with its images of defeat, the death wish, the psychiatrist's couch, the hangman's shed? Or only half-true? At least recognizable.

In spite of the dark negations of these poems, which we faithfully read, the students took a fancy to a word omitted there. A plain monosyllable (still in the language, not yet antique), they liked the sound of poetry in it—"Yes." In the "Age of Anxiety," Malin calls it man's tragedy that he is "unwilling to say Yes."

I would advise any writer who wants to be endorsed by the young in heart to work it into his remarks. I don't mean its terse use in Addison's essay "Leonora's Library": "I answered *Yes,* for I hate long speeches. . . ." I mean electing the affirmatives, from time to time saying yes instead of no, like the final words of Joyce's *Ulysses:* "And yes I said yes I will Yes."

They found the word in Hopkins, "I did say yes O at lightning and lashed rod," only to discover that Cummings, in taking up the refrain, had practically appropriated it. He must have nodded his head all his life.

> Out of the lie of no
> rises a truth of yes.

"We'll make yes," he said. "Yes is a world." "yes is a pleasant country." "around we go yes." Yes is the moon "much too busy being her beautiful yes." Yes is the lovers whose eyes "would never miss a yes." "as yes is to if, love is to yes." "and pure so now and now so yes." "forgetting if, remember yes." "wish by spirit and if by yes,"

and everybody never breathed
quite so many kinds of yes

A good word, yes. "Whatever it is, let it be without affectation," agreed Marianne Moore, "Yes, yes, yes, *yes.*" Even the timid students too menaced by the hellgazers to trust it entirely or expect any positive joy on this futile planet were quick to go partway and agree to the idea of tragic joy (yes, isn't life terrible?), as Yeats best defined it —we begin to live only when we realize that life is a tragedy, accepting the murderousness with a gaiety which transfigures the dread.

They liked the proposition that life is sweet no matter how grinding the terms. If poets bemoaning a fragmented world unfortunately made sense, then others who felt at home in the ruins made more. It was better to emit a joyful noise, a student said, "at the sight of one's own suffering."

They would be content like Yeats, they thought, to live it all again and yet again. Yeats offered them the gift of his fierce joy. Beyond this, if there was one sweeping line of poetry they would remember above the rest it was Dylan Thomas's, "Oh, isn't life a terrible thing, thank God!" I saw to that.

"The thing perhaps is," said Cummings, "to eat flowers and not to be afraid."

"The thing to do," said a student, "is to keep a stiff upper chin."

I told them poetry was indispensable, and they looked respectful. Some wrote it hurriedly in their notebooks. I might have added Cocteau's words, "I know that poetry is indispensable, but I do not know for what."

Maybe it was useful to tell them in what direction they should go, that is, to escape the disaster areas and the wasteland.

"We must all go, each in his own direction," said Eliot in *The Family Reunion,* not very helpful in pointing out the route. What port or haven? Which is the way of the quester?

Not long ago a Southern lady whom I know set off alone on a journey and, while driving her car over strange roads, stopped at a fork uncertain which road to take. She took the left fork, then in doubt called out to a man working on construction there.

"Am I going in the right direction?" she shouted.

He thought a minute. "Where is it you want to go, lady?"

The right direction—that narrowed the choice somewhat, avoiding the aimless and the arbitrary, eliminating possibly the wrong direction. One might go in quest of salvation, as Eliot suggested, a journey to take as one could: on muleback or raft, wheelbarrow or camel, by safari or rabbit chase, though Eliot went by the dark night of the soul. After reading his play, a student found another route: "It is interesting to note that to reach salvation one must start with a cocktail party."

The trip promised to be exhausting, however you set about it. For lack of better there was Theodore Roethke's method: "I learn by going where I have to go." But how do you know when you get there?

One might seek Eliot's still center, Yeats's Byzantium, or Auden's Just City (like Bunyan's Celestial City or St. Augustine's City of God), even if Auden himself lost his ticket and his vocation, a lapsed quester, and abandoned the search. Or there was Kafka's unattainable castle. The Kafka motif, I confess, seemed to run through my own meanders, ending predictably with the loss of the castle. I never did have a good sense of direction, especially in a dream landscape. Besides, the quest as such was hardly meant for women, who make poor knights-errant. What in my bones did I know of the chivalric ideal or the need to go traipsing after the Holy Grail?

Furthermore, one couldn't always distinguish quest from flight. Were they the same thing: escape and exile, a fleeing *from* (as Eliot, Pound, and Auden fled their native lands, crossing the ocean in opposite directions)? Or was the quest after all a search for a solution, such as for meaning, certainty, God, love, peace, or oneself?

On a train trip B. and I took once from Vienna to Ostend, a map of the route contained the words, *"confort, tranquillité, et repos,"* adding in English, "a troublefree journey." This was, I think, the ultimate aim of the quest. A journey with no end.

In the classroom, however, my time-racked mind stayed necessarily on the clock, which watched me, to get the quest over and done by 10:10 A.M. Neither a glimpse of timelessness nor a promise of eternity would hold the students like birds of passage a minute overtime. With the clock I went round in circles. The chiding bell rang, it was too late for deliverance, we were mortal flesh fifty minutes older, circling to decay. Infinitude could wait till next week.

A quicker method might have been one of visual aid resorted to by a professor in a mathematics class. He drew a white chalk line across the blackboard and with a flourish threw the chalk out of the open window.

"That's infinity," he said.

Yet with the dire need of quest agreed upon, few poets encouraged staying quietly at home, though the traffic grew dense, the routes and airlanes overloaded. Questers nearly collided from too much flight. Wallace Stevens was kind enough to limit his search to this planet, rejecting heaven or hell as luckily nonexistent. Eliot's still center might do for Eliot, not for Stevens, to whom it was no more real than God's Heaven of pearly gates and gold pavements. In truth Eliot's paradise, inspired by Dante and St. John of the Cross, resembled a rose garden with singing birds, fountains, yew trees, shafts of sunlight, and the laughter of children. Stevens viewed it with a shrug, asking in effect, "You mean Eden? But *this,* sir, is Eden!" This earth was our garden, unsponsored by any God, to Stevens all of paradise we need or we shall know.

Cummings too was content with the pursuit of his own temporal world of spring and the mating season, from which mostpeople were excluded because mostpeople are not human beings. You and I are human beings. We are glad and young, we consent to life. They are impersons in an inhuman unworld. They are manunkind, a hopeless case, part of the unmystery. They are the undead in "a world so unso." They exist by negation. They give only unlove. The failure in life is the failure of love.

You and I need but say Yes to get inside Cummings's island of rejoicing. He had arrived where he wanted to be, where "whatever sages say and fools, all's well," where love is, where "love is the every only god."

But it would be patently absurd to reject mostpeople, including senior professors, on the grounds that they lacked an appreciation for poetry. A professor of sociology at Duke, invited one afternoon to join a discussion group, told the students, "If I were the father of a son, I'd rather have him be a ballet dancer than a poet. In either case I'd disown him as a pansy."

Had he by chance been reading John Locke, who found much to say against a son wasting his time making verses? If the boy revealed a poetic vein, said Locke (mixing his metaphor and stifling a vein in the process), it should be stifled at once and suppressed.

The professor started no argument. No one rose to defend poetry for not being a treatise in sociology. As students will, in their tact they listened, offered him a cup of coffee, and let him run on unrebuked with (as George Eliot said of a professor in *Middlemarch*) "the perfect liberty of misjudgement." He was a literalist. He belonged to the H. L. Mencken school of critics, and like Mencken (who boasted having a highly literal mind and a lifelong distrust of poetry) condemned poems as "pretty little bellyaches." Without reading them, the professor knew what poets were, obscure, precious, unintelligible (an observation often demonstrably true). To him they were spouters, they weren't masculine, they spoke in whines, bleats, and self-pity. A man had a duty to protect the virility of his son (if he had a son).

In fairness I wondered at the time, what did I know or care about sociology? It dealt—didn't it?—with human groups and their patterns of social behavior, their love relationships. Could anyone have convinced me of its virtue, its ability to change and glorify my life?

Still, it was wonderful to think of the awestruck cry of Hopkins, for example, as a bellyache.

Poetry is indispensable, I told them, and so are the poets. I admit I did not know for what, unless to

> Make tigers tame, and huge leviathans
> Forsake unsounded deeps to dance on sands.

Take Hopkins. One morning at breakfast I read in the newspaper, during some extreme world crisis, that this was the most dangerous hour in the history of the human race. "We are a nation in anxious doubt," it said, bent on our own destruction, unable to save ourselves. I've forgotten which crisis, perhaps the Korean. Or the Suez. Or the Berlin. Or the Cuban. There have been so many.

At 9:20 in class we were reading aloud Hopkins's poems: "The world is charged with the grandeur of God." "I walk, I lift up, I lift up heart, eyes, Down all that glory in the heavens to glean our Saviour."

This was a man living in a God-centered world, where merely to lift one's eyes was to see manifest the shining proof of that redeeming presence. In the skies, hills, earth, like a lover to be adored, Christ offered himself, "Here am I!" Hopkins the beholder was half hurled off his feet with tidings of joy.

It crossed my mind what queer reading this made, hard to call reliable or timely in the midst of world blunder, with tidings that scarcely matched the chilling headlines.

It was ironical, like reciting the opening lines of "The Waste Land" one April morning during the wettest downpour of the season: "April is the cruellest month,"

> And the dead tree gives no shelter, the cricket no relief,
> And the dry stone no sound of water . . .

The wasteland was actually awash. We were drowning in Eliot's drought. The girls had left their gaudy open umbrellas in wet clusters outside the classroom door, like April in a tulip garden. Hadn't anybody caught on that it was *raining* outdoors?

Nor did the shine of God last for Hopkins, so what imperishable lesson abided there? He too found the world was too much with him. He too, "a lonely began," entered the dark night where he stumbled and groped, lost and forsaken, calling "Comforter, where, where is your comforting?" Darkness closed in as night follows day—the hour of reckoning, the night of wrath—and he was unmanned and unselved. God had become the enemy, turned his back, withdrawn, abandoned him.

> I am gall, I am heartburn. God's most deep decree
> Bitter would have me taste: my taste was *me*.

"Poetry makes nothing happen," said Auden in his elegy to Yeats. It makes nothing happen, yet it is indispensable. It expresses our world (does it?) in which war is constant and man has conquered the moon. William Carlos Williams thought so:

The province of the poem is the world.
When the sun rises, it rises in the poem
And when it sets darkness comes down
And the poem is dark . . .
                                    —"Paterson," III

Marianne Moore called poetry "all this fiddle." Wallace Stevens had to snicker at "Such tink and tank and tunk-a-tunk-tunk." Both of them wrote the stuff steadily all their lives.

Miss Moore worried me as too fastidious and ladylike, too fey a writer in a quaking world. She preferred a zoo or bestiary. Yet her discovery that animals were cleverer than men at survival, while unnerving, made plenty of sense. A wise animal wore armor to protect itself, went spiked and battle-dressed, wary and austere, with the quills of a porcupine, the armor of the armadillo. Jellyfish knew how to sting. The elephant had the hide of a cocoanut shell. The anteater while non-aggressive wore "sting-proof scales." Carried away by her respect for skunks—those noble little warriors—only they, she said, "shall associate with me." (But how wide was her acquaintance?)

It was sheer animal wisdom before engulfing calamity to contract like the snail and withdraw one's horns, learn to survive without water like the desert rat, be ready to run like the ostrich. The best thing about a rose was its thorns. Of the cactus she cried, "What is there like fortitude!"

To be stoical, detached, solitary, unmolested, to adjust to rigors like the reindeer, defend oneself with claws like the mongoose—this was her advice for survival in our time. When I read her I thought of Lepidus befuddled by wine asking Antony, "What manner o' thing is your crocodile? . . . 'Tis a strange serpent."

Antony: " 'Tis so. And the tears of it are wet."

77

Miss Moore wore the plate armor of spinsterhood, which however protective of her person was a little too spiked and heavy for me. She was more kin than I to the arctic ox (or goat) of whom she spoke approving, "so some decide to stay unwed."

D. H. Lawrence, on the other hand, looked with greater latitude at the same natural world and saw only sex. "My sex is *me*," he wrote, "and nobody will make me feel shame about it," a distinction he shared with the elephant and the tortoise. As a student figured it out, "He was obsessed by sex, or something of that type."

If Miss Moore's chaste menagerie had a strict morality to teach, Lawrence's had none. He found so much sexual significance in the birds, beasts, and flowers that he wrote a book *Birds, Beasts, and Flowers,* followed by *Pansies* and *More Pansies*. He examined, with no sense of overdoing it, the pomegranate, fig, peach, grape, and pansy, along with the bat, mosquito, kangaroo, hummingbird and she-goat ("And when the billy goat mounts her She is brittle as brimstone"), reporting them amorous and sexy, especially the turtle—six poems on the mating of turtles and turtle love:

> Making his advances
> He does not look at her, nor sniff at her,
> No, not even sniff at her, his nose is blank.

Instead, he catches her trouser-legs in his beak and drags her along like a dog. "We ought to look the other way," said Lawrence (so we ought),

> Save that, having come with you so far,
> We will go on to the end.

Lawrence had a cow, Black-Eyed Susan, with whom he fell (platonically) in love. "There *is* a sort of relation be-

tween us. And this relation is part of the mystery of love. . . .
The queer cowy mystery of her is her changeless cowy
desirableness." As he milked her or gazed into her eyes, he
thought, "Is not this my life, this throbbing of the bull's
blood in my blood?"

The message was clear: lust, Lawrence's sweet lyre of
lust. So man ought to behave. "For man as for flower and
beast and bird, the supreme triumph is to be most vividly,
most perfectly alive . . . in the flesh."

This too, I suppose, was the poetry of survival.

Love being indispensable, the theme had endless varia-
tions. How could the poets, melodists of love, in reason agree
about what it is? (Reason and love keep little company
together nowadays, Bottom observed.) They ranged from
William Carlos Williams's claim, "Love's very fleas are mine"
to Eliot's dismal measure in Sweeney's words—"Birth, copulation, and death. That's all, that's all, that's all, that's all,"
and his girlfriend Doris's tired reply, "I'd be bored"—to the
incantatory "hell over bells" kind of love celebrated by
Dylan Thomas in the Welsh village of Llareggub: "The
town's as full as a lovebird's egg." *Bugger all* is Llareggub
backward, but I think he meant it kindly.

Thomas conducted a love festival in *Under Milk Wood*.
While Mr. Utah Watkins's cow (like Lawrence's) kissed him
and mooed tender words, love among mortals burgeoned as
it would: in the prudent yearning of Mog Edwards and
Myfanwy Price; the happy bawdy married love of Mr. and
Mrs. Cherry Owen; the wornout love of Mr. and Mrs. Pugh
become murder in the heart; the love of Man and God in
Rev. Eli Jenkins; the dream of love in ripe young maidens
like Mae Rose Cottage and Gossamer Beynon ("Spring stirs
Gossamer Beynon like a spoon").

Most eloquent was Polly Garter's total love, the town

prostitute who loved them all, Tom, Dick, and Harry, knowing that life was a ribald and terrible thing, thank God, that men must have love to survive, that she could give what she had to give. And there was Dylan Thomas's love, who wrote about it.

You could depend upon the poets to be contrary, seldom in accord, every man in his humor, out of humor with the rest. Thomas said his poetry recorded a struggle from darkness to light. Hopkins struggled undone from light to darkness. Eliot said the light and the dark were the same thing.

A poet freely contradicted even himself. Yeats described the way a poem comes right with a click like a closing box, then kept on forever rewriting his own. Ezra Pound had a paralyzing ego, the id of the century, the most relentlessly vain man of our time. Yet he wrote the beautiful lyric, "Pull down thy vanity, I say pull down." At a meeting of the Rhymers Club in London he ate the tulips on the table to attract attention. He wore trousers of bright green billiard cloth, pink coat, blue shirt, hand-painted tie, sombrero, flaming red beard, a single turquoise earring, and a strut. Little Black Sambo. Yet this show-off, Pound-foolish poet wrote

> Learn of the green world
> What can be thy place.
> Pull down thy vanity.

The students accommodated them all, or most of them. And so did I. Thoreau knew this to be true: "The question is not what you look at, but what you see." A poet possessed a witnessing eye. More than that, he had his own slant or focus, a way of seeing what he saw. A way of looking was a way of being. It might reveal him in the end squint-eyed, cockeyed, clear-sighted, or visionary. Seldom did it show him blind.

The failure in mostpeople, it seemed, was not to see or hear anything. By a poet Wallace Stevens meant merely a man who *saw*, any man of imagination, like Crispin,

> Crispin beheld, and Crispin was made new.

Stevens, the man with the blue guitar, played a tune about the look of things as they are and, as best he could, "a tune beyond." "I have been trying to see the world about me," he said in a letter, "both as I see it and as it is."

> He held the world upon his nose
> And this-a-way he gave a fling.
>
> His robes and symbols, ai-yi-yi—
> And that-a-way he twirled the thing.

This balancing act marked him for a clown but an aspiring clown—a poet. No wonder there are so few poets in the history of man. The wonder is a few have stayed immortal till now.

Yeats found poetry indispensable to become acquainted with Yeats. His scanning of self-affairs provided a vigorous defense of poetry. Through it he made the momentous discovery (or thought he did), "So this is I."

A man who narrowly escaped from fairyland, he sought the company and finer knowledge of Yeats—what manner of Irishman, the nature of his trade—thereby hoping to wither into the truth with the vital issue at stake: "It is *myself* that I remake." He sought his identity in a walking-naked enterprise. But then, so did Montaigne.

It meant dropping the early romantic pose, leaving behind a dream world of Celtic twilight. Instead he looked at "the reality," the events of his life, the people in it—how it felt to be in love with a political agitator, soapbox orator, fanatic, and dedicated revolutionary who preached violence and overthrow of government. It felt awful. Maud Gonne drove him mad, rejecting his love for love of the Cause, which was Ireland, "my fool-driven land," choosing to marry that "drunken, vainglorious lout," Major John MacBride, who was finally executed for his part in the terrible comedy.

All his life Yeats loved a woman who didn't love him. For poetry's sake she may have been wise to be unattainable. What, though, did Yeats learn in the process about Yeats? When he sought the truth about himself, he found many conflicting versions of self. Even a naked man wore diadems and masks. He went in motley for the masquerade.

Yet before he died at seventy-four he wrote in a letter: "It seems to me that I have found what I wanted. When I try to put all into a phrase I say, 'Man can embody truth but he cannot know it.' " Man can live with it, taste, see, hear, feel it, without knowing what it is.

This human limitation Yeats obligingly demonstrated. Even in his epitaph, which he spelled out with care shortly before his death—so late, so late, he managed to foul it up and get the wording wrong:

> Cast a cold eye
> On life, on death.
> Horseman, pass by!

What prompted him to say that? A slip of the pen? He must have meant instead "Cast a hot eye," for he was in fact a hotblooded man of flesh, a foolish passionate man, a wild old wicked man in love with sex, who clung to this earth and the lecheries of life, this "blind man's ditch," this "rag-and-bone shop of the heart," and never let go. That was the way Yeats looked at life and death.

However facile his juggling of the truth, with the insight

of the young the students were on his side, taking him at his word including the lunatic part: Yeats the dabbler in magic, augury, astrology, mysticism, spiritualism, reincarnation, theosophy and the occult, a fortuneteller, communicator with ghosts, and all that.

"Yeats was not a hypocrite," one said in extenuation. "He had dual ideas."

"Reading Yeats," said another, "I experienced a flight of the imagination."

T. S. Eliot knew poetry to be indispensable, indeed meaningless *unless* it could be put to use and applied directly to existence. A poet wrote to make a difference in our lives. A poet stood as interpreter, erring but necessary.

I was useful too as interpreter of the poet. He couldn't make a difference in a student's life, or in mine, till we knew what he was saying in what tone of voice. Without meaning, the poem wasn't visible. It wasn't *there*. I spent years of my life extracting Eliot, who I think owed me a debt for being so cooperative, roundly though he denounced the lemon-squeezer school of critics.

At least one student defended me: "We have to squeeze the lemons. How else can we hope to get any juice out of him?"

The joke was grisly when Eliot died (in 1965) that the journalists could recall only how he had mouthed something about the way the world ends—not with a bang but a whimper. As a final twist of the knife, they quoted these as the last words of "The Waste Land," when the last prayerful word of that poem, as anyone knows who reads him, is *Shantih*—peace, peace, peace, a cry to catch God's ear.

So I told them, like Matthew Arnold, that the future of poetry was immense. When Robert Lowell was asked a century after Arnold about the future of poetry, he said, "I don't know. It's a very dark crystal." One could say the same thing, with equal justice, about the future of the world.

Since the university had become, by default or by opening its doors, nearly the only refuge left for poetry in our time, the last sanctuary, the poets hastened to us in person, works in hand. Each fall and spring a poet or two arrived at Duke to give a "poetry reading" and vent his views, though we did not, as many colleges did, acquire a poet-in-residence. It was too unbuttoned an idea for Duke to subsidize a poet just to sit around and write poems and talk. Except for Dylan Thomas and E. E. Cummings, these live and viable poets in our midst seemed in general to do more harm than good.

In past centuries, from Chaucer to Thomas Hardy, the poet seldom would be caught teaching. I suppose it didn't occur to him as his vocation, or that he had words to spare or anything pedantic to say. Now his audience consisted of a row of college students plus a few loyal professors. Like most poets on the lecture platform (Auden, Lowell, Wilbur, Eberhart, Jarrell, Roethke, Shapiro, Dickey), he was pretty sure to be a professor himself, or a librarian like Philip Larkin, a frightening state of affairs. Poetry was being written by teachers and taught by poets. It had become, of all things, academic.

Cummings protested he wasn't a teacher but a learner, an ignoramus, an individual, whose blood approved of being wholly a fool. Yet he gave six *nonlectures* to students during a year spent at Harvard, then went about the country to colleges that invited him and gave more, teaching his head off ("That fool could be so deep contemplative"), telling us what and what not to think, lecturing on his own lower-case *i*. As for the ego required for such revelations of self, "Who," he inquired, "if i may be so inconsiderate as to ask, isn't egocentric?"

Cummings contrived to be charmingly persuasive. He sounded like somebody who endorsed being, yes, alive. The great advantage in being alive instead of undying, he said (speaking from a totally biased and entirely personal point of view),

> —the great (my darling) happens to be
> that love are in we, that love are in we

Dylan Thomas could have filled the outdoor stadium. A little, beery man with curly hair, snub nose, pot belly, he sweated and chain-smoked, and his voice was magical enough to make you believe you listened to harps or harpies and angels. Since he began his reading with a prose piece, "A Visit to America," a vulgar, windy, ill-natured attack on America (how he had "swigged and guzzled" over here, how he had lectured to "rich minked chunks of American matron-hood"), and since a number of students swooned to hear him and mistook this prate for the rarest poetry, I suppose it didn't matter much *what* he read.

"I hate reading my poems aloud," Dylan Thomas told me in sad apology on that May night's visit to Duke, six months before his death. He was unassuming in private talk, shamed by his role of public poet, with too few poems so far to his name. (But he would rewrite a single line fifty to a hundred times.) He said his words reproached him from the platform: "Whenever I read a poem, it looks up at me from the page and says, 'Fool! Why don't you go back to work?' "

It was the bad poets, however, the small nameless minor maundering poets scurrying past on their way to oblivion, who did the real harm. They made poetry ridiculous. They chanted their unpublished works in hushed cathedral tones, pausing at the arbitrary end of line to lean on the mortified air and let the syllables float away. They spoke in howls or cryptograms, or murmured to themselves what nobody could hear or understand. They bared their breasts and departed. All that delirium of the brave.

John Ciardi has advised, "Do not demand that a poem be more rational than you are." I've no idea why not? But these were less rational than we were, and we knew it. Too often a poet's wares were shoddy and dross. They showed us the way poetry was going, to the dogs. So the students, though patient, grew restless and skeptical, then resentful. We lost ground.

Somebody remarked one night in compassion for a passing poet, "Well, he tried."

I could only ask in amazement, "Tried *what?*"

I felt aggrieved when a poet made a bad show. To support the muse, it was needful to bind her wounds, hold her up by the ears. One had to be her friend and testifier, her steady advocate. Yet I found it impossible to distinguish these multitudinous young poets from each other, to recall their faces or tell them apart. One night in a dream my poetry class asked, "Tell us about Mr. Cholesterol." "Oh oh," I thought, "which new poet is that?"

"Poetry isn't very likely to save the world, is it?" said a student after a poetry reading. In a century of wars, poetry had faced the same problem of survival. It had fought its bloody own, lost in the thick of battle, corpses lining the roadside.

"No, I shouldn't think so," I said. "It may reflect our world and its rhythms, that's all."

"And who will care?"

"You and I."

VI

⟫⟫⟫⟫⟫⟫⟫⟫⟫⟫⟫⟫⟫⟫⟪⟪⟪⟪⟪⟪⟪⟪⟪⟪⟪⟪⟪⟪

Following two years behind David, Philip at fifteen went in his turn to Exeter. We had no children left, only two boys away at school. B.'s habits and mine returned to the casual ones before they were born, with the addition of a cocktail before dinner and an ever-growing passion for each other's company. On the days I stayed at home instead of teaching, B. telephoned three or four times from his office. "I wanted to hear the sound of your voice, love."

Any time of day or night he could have told where I was— at 10:30 A.M. Tuesday, say, "She's in her classroom, 108 Carr, talking about John Donne, 'The Ecstasy.'" At 11:20, "Let's see. She should be walking down the hall of Carr Building, probably with a student, on her way to the library." Or I could have said, at 3:50 P.M. of a Friday, "I think you'll find him putting on his coat. In ten minutes he has a meeting of the Faculty Council."

Philip at Exeter wrote he was "busy as a tinker's damn," offering the wistful reason, "Not many dames up here." He received Honors in his first term, an A in mathematics and a D in physics (he is now a nuclear physicist), and joined the Rifle Club, where as rifleman he was presented by the United States Government with a medal that said "Small Bore." In May he gave a lecture to the school on Relativity.

David entered Harvard in September. Against our will, he had applied to join the NROTC unit (from a desire to lessen our expenses, though both boys had earned scholarships each year), and now he was sworn in as midshipman with $50 a month pay from the Navy, wearing a uniform, learning to drill, studying under Commander Hughes the science of killing in a course called "Naval Weapons." On his first training cruise in the summer of 1949, they assigned him to gunnery on the battleship *Missouri* (where the Japanese surrender in World War II was signed). His gunfiring station as powder hoist was on the sixteen-inch turret No. 2. He was also pointer on a five-inch gun mount, aiming at target.

I hated it violently, with a sickened heart. I hated it so much I lay awake nights composing a letter to President Conant of Harvard, "Dear President Conant: This is one hell of a way to run a railroad." It was the farthest I got in my complaint, but the words were reproachful. I don't know why I held him personally responsible for the tottering state of things—running a military school where students were taught the art of fighting the next war—but I couldn't very well write, expecting a reply, the Secretary of the Navy or the Pentagon.

I might better have phrased it, "This is one hell of a way to run a world." Or, in the quaint words of Samuel Beckett: "Christ, what a planet!"

Yet on shore leave David saw Paris that summer, on foot, as B. and I had done twenty years before. As we had, he liked best the Impressionists at the Jeu de Paume, and the church of St. Sulpice. He went to Montmartre late one night after a walk in the Bois de Boulogne, witnessed as he said "the open and shameless bargaining for love," and tramped the miles back to his hotel in aching, stocking feet to save the price of a cab. It was uncanny. He had no way of knowing that B. and I, when young, had done the same thing.

I said to B., "We never told him. How did he happen to do exactly what we did?"

B. said, "Everybody does."

"No," I said. Not everybody. Only Bevingtons.

The boys were forever gone, the house was empty. I read in a newspaper column the question: "Can you love your children too much?" and asked B. his opinion.

"Yes, I suppose so," he said.

"Wrong!" I said. "It says here you can't: 'You can't love anyone too much.' " You could only love them and let them go.

We had no reason now to stay home from Senegal or Pago Pago. Since B. was due to take a year's sabbatical leave, he invited me to request a leave of absence without pay, which I instantly did. I had been promoted to the rank of assistant professor two years ago, but the University was not prepared so soon to pay me to disappear for fifteen months, not even on "compassionate" leave.

It seemed urgent to go away, anywhere, and take a deep breath. Two people had died in the past few months whose deaths were an unbearable event that left me haunted and reduced, unsure in a world so much the worse. Both times the word had come by telephone.

One call was from my half-brother Boyce in Chicago, a man I scarcely knew whose voice I didn't recognize, with the incredible news of Charley.

"Charley's dead," Boyce told me. "He died this morning."

"*Who?*" I asked. "What do you mean, Charley?"

"I mean our father."

I had never in my life lived with Charley, beyond a matter of a few months, since the time my mother divorced him when I was two years old. I should have thought it wouldn't matter greatly to me whether he lived or died.

The loss was unexpected and terrible, the defeat of hope,

the final giving up of something I had never had. His beautiful singing voice pounded like the sea in my ears— "Jerusalem, Jerusalem, lift up your gates and sing!"—why must I hear him shouting that old song now? Time had reached a stop, too late for love. Charley would not get around to loving me after all, or explain his side of the story (if he ever intended to), why it was I had been unclaimed. I had no father. The loss was final and the hurt real.

Only a few days earlier, Fanny Patton had telephoned, with shock and grief in her voice. "Then you haven't heard? Newman White died last night of a heart attack."

If Henry Adams was right in his elevated—some would say limited—view of friendship ("One friend in a lifetime is much. Two are many. Three are hardly possible"), then Newman White was my friend.

These were the first deaths, really the first to call a part and prophecy of my own death.

On the September day when we sailed for England on the *Mauretania,* classes began at Duke without us and the English pound was devalued from $4.03 to $2.80. By handing us a bucketful of dollars, Sir Stafford Cripps, Chancellor of the Exchequer, made us unexpectedly welcome. I regretted my habit of referring to him, because of a radio announcer's spoonerism, as Sir Stifford Craps.

Arriving at Waterloo Station, we went straight out to Hampstead on the London Underground and moved in that night with the Jørgensens at 4 Holford Road. They were a goodhearted Danish couple our own age, who occupied the second and third floors of a large brick house just off Hampstead Heath, and rented out a couple of rooms to persons who took their fancy. Being aliens (like us) in a strange land, rebuffed by neighbors, they were lonely and wanted company.

Charles Ward, in the English Department at Duke, had spent a year living with the Jørgensens and winning their love. Charles had recommended us to follow him. The other occupant besides us was Edgar Shannon, a slangy young bachelor from Harvard, in London to write a book on Tennyson's reviewers, who has since become President of the University of Virginia. One sees therefore that the Jørgensens' standards were laudable but abnormally high. They had an innocent faith in the intellect, which led to a touching weakness for American professors.

We were blessed by accident, counted among the elect. In bombed-out London, after four years still war-torn from World War II, a place of ravage, austerity, and strict rationing, we ate with the Jørgensens, who somehow managed to spirit eggs, butter, and an occasional joint out of Denmark. We drank with the Jørgensens, who began each night's bountiful dinner with aquavit and continued with Danish beer. Most of all, we heard from them which way the wind was blowing.

Jørgensen was a newspaper man, a foreign correspondent for five newspapers in Denmark. He came home each night from attending the sessions of the House of Commons, from gathering the news on Fleet Street, and at dinner cried havoc, relaying to us the latest disasters. We were the first of the populace to know, if that was a privilege. At 9:00 P.M. we sat beside him to hear the broadcast over again, word for word but without the tirade, on the B.B.C. News. It was weird how accurate and knowledgeable he was (as he readily agreed), not to add how opinionated and scrappy. We had the state of the collapsing world interpreted, analyzed, and dusted off by an expert, who never got his facts wrong, only on occasion, like any man, his conclusions.

A melancholy Dane, with a lively wit and eloquence second only to Winston Churchill's, like Churchill he would have expired without an audience. Typically he seldom listened to a reply. One might have changed the subject to talk of the castrati or early Biedermeier without his hearing a word.

"I've had it," he would begin the evening report of chaos, shaking his head and rumpling his gray hair in the deepest gloom. "By God, this time, *this* time I've *had* it!"

Clement Attlee as mousy Prime Minister of the Labour Government, we learned, was pushing England to the edge of bankruptcy. The next war, almost upon us, would burst out any day in Korea between the Republic in the South and the Communist-controlled regime in the North. China had fallen on September 21 to the Communists, when Red China was born and Mao Tse-tung, like Stalin, became a dictator. Communism was the last thundercrack, the warning rumble of the breaking up of the planet.

On the night of September 23, Jørgensen brought home word of an atomic explosion inside Russia, fearful proof that behind the Iron Curtain they had the secret of the bomb. On November 6 he told us that Malenkov in Moscow charged America with preparing to unleash a third World War.

He sounded like Churchill, who had inquired of Parliament, "What is Europe now?" and answered himself: "It is a rubble-heap, a charnel house, a breeding ground of pestilence and hate." I wondered if we should take the next ship home.

When the news ran out, Jørgensen chilled us with one more lurid episode from World War I, when he had been wounded, gassed, and shell-shocked. Or from World War II, when he had risked his life daily in the underground movement of sabotage against the German occupation. That recent blow-up was in Copenhagen. Now in London he awaited in a fume the repetition of cataclysm—with England caught in the middle of an East-West conflict, a head-on clash to the finish between two rival supernations mad for power, both possessing nuclear missiles to destroy the world: America and Stalin's Russia, the US and the USSR. Jørgensen grew so bellicose the marvel was he didn't throw us out of the house.

"I've had it up to here," he groaned. "A lifetime of war! Haven't you bloody idiots sense enough to know we've *had* it?"

And B. would weary of the doomful talk. "He tickles my catastrophe," he said in the privacy of our room.

Mrs. Jørgensen looked like Monet's amiable "Madame Paul," wife of a pastry cook, her mind full of sugarplums. Out in the kitchen, while Edgar and I wiped the dishes, the talk with jolly, plump, brown-haired Mrs. Jørgensen grew merrier as she harped on her favorite topics: how to put up with the stuffy English, how to find Edgar an American wife.

"But you must never, never kiss her in public," she said. "Nice people don't do that. It isn't nice."

"Not even on New Year's Eve?" we asked.

She had nothing against Americans except their unbridled appetite for kissing, Coca-Cola, and Kraft process cheese. She didn't agree with her husband they might be getting ready to throw a bomb at her.

B.'s first move was to buy a car from Dagenham Motors on Park Lane, a tacky secondhand Anglia they would have blushed to exhibit in their showrooms—a mite-sized, eight-horsepower Ford that got forty miles to the gallon and nipped along like a little black sewing machine or a London taxicab. I laughed every time I climbed into it, that is, I laughed if B. remembered to drive on the left-hand side of the road. When we purred up the High Street, Hampstead, and turned at the tube station into steep, narrow Heath Street, he inclined to swing neatly to the right lane. Once an aged pedestrian on the sidewalk witnessed this wilful, unlawful behavior, which made him hysterical. He bobbed up and down wringing his hands, muttering, "Oh dear, dear, dear, oh dear me!"

Few cars were on the road, since with rationing only the rare Londoner was permitted to buy a car or the petrol to run one. Through Mr. Francis of the British Museum, we were allowed enough petrol to drive back and forth from Hampstead to Bloomsbury, six miles, with a few gallons left over for literary excursions on the weekend.

Down through Camden Town past Regent's Park, I used to brood about me at scarred London, the ruin left by bombs and burning, and wonder what Henry James would think of these woeful blemishes now—these "town-vistas" he called the most romantic in the world. He thought London the headquarters of the English tongue (where one needn't associate with base vocables) and the capital of the human race (barring a few disfigurements, such as the mean slum houses, "so many rows of coal-scuttles," or the "vulgar little railing" of Green Park). Henry James, fastidious man, had looked at Edwardian London over the apron of a hansom cab. What would he say to the vulgarity of this malign destruction, these gaping, inelegant wounds?

Over 700,000 houses had been damaged or destroyed. Yet amid the rubble—the charred wood, broken plaster, twisted iron pipes, the cracked and leaning buildings, the jagged halves of dwellings, the ruined cellars—grew the red geraniums. They bloomed that autumn row on row in the bomb sites, a gaudy and defiant flowering, reflecting what had been done to England, what could never be done. They were like Churchill's V sign for victory. They denied the ugly truth with an air of smartening up the dooryard, another English garden planted in the open spaces.

When we had a glimpse of Mr. Churchill early in November, he resembled a red geranium himself. At Grosvenor House one morning he put in a belated appearance at the Sunday *Times* Book Exhibition to receive the year's award for the second volume of his memoirs of World War II. A full two hours before his arrival, the ground floor of Grosvenor House was jammed. Two gentlewomen fainted and were carried out, and we stood crushed together in— since it was England—stoic and politely enduring silence.

At last a small procession advanced to the place of ceremony, in its midst a roly-poly Leader of the Opposition, so genuinely rotund, so cherubic, one thought with pleasure of the moonface advertised on London buses: "Guinness is good for you."

There was a round of mild applause. Then from all sides of the impassive crowd came exclamations of approval and esteem, a love murmur of praise. "Oh-h-h, the old *dear!*" whispered the housewives, eyes aglisten. "There's a love, that one, a lovely man!" Huskily, the stolid husbands whispered too, "Hear, hear."

"It's Mr. Churchill," the stranger next to me explained with a catch in his voice.

We stilled ourselves to listen. Churchill beamed about him at ease and opened his mouth to speak, saying nothing but declaiming much. For ten minutes he spun out words with abundant grace, authority, eloquence, and humor, in flawlessly rounded periods, the King's English carved and polished into Churchill's own.

Coming to a pause, the end of his improvisation, he drew from his pocket a newspaper clipping that had quoted him on a similar occasion. While we waited expectant, he took time to glance through it over his horn-rimmed spectacles and, finding it well put, read it to us again. He raised his pudgy hand, smiled a beatific farewell. "Then-kyou," he said, and left.

On a Sunday afternoon in November, B. and I emerged at dusk blinded from gazing at Turner's steamy sunrises in the National Gallery at Trafalgar Square.

"Look, it's raining, it's pouring!" I cried, holding out my hand. No rain fell from the leaden sky. Beyond our heads were hundreds and hundreds of starlings, wintering in London, perched crowded together on the Greek cornices and Corinthian porticos, lining each horizontal ledge under the eaves. They were gusty as a tempest. Their twitter was like hailstones, like the pelting sleet of a winter storm.

Over Trafalgar Square a ballet of starlings was being performed. Above Lord Nelson's monument—himself (a little man) seventeen feet tall at its top—thousands of passerine birds moved in sweeping flight climbing, wheeling over St. Martin's, rising and descending on Charing Cross in rhythmic unison about the sky. They were thick as the leaves in Vallombrosa. The world was black with a procession of starlings.

On the sidewalk across from the National Gallery, a child stopped under a plane tree and clapped his hands. With a swishing movement upward, a swarm of glossy black birds emptied the tree, lifting higher and higher on pointed wings. The boy ran to the next tree and clapped again. We stood laughing on the museum steps, then walked to the Embankment where, beside the Thames till night fell, we stopped occasionally to clap our hands. And the starlings streamed up like bullets from the treetops in wide, ever-darkening circles of flight.

Hampstead was a hill village, with a High Street and Christchurch peal of bells. At the peak of the steep hill, where we lived, the Heath began. The village on the next hill was Highgate. Amazingly, B. and I could walk to our street corner and at White Stone Pond (where Shelley sailed his paper boats) plunge into the Heath, in five minutes out of sight of London as if it didn't exist. We strolled in woods on leafy paths. We lay in the grass, put our ear to the ground, and heard no city sound at all.

I loved it best in November, when the fogs and mists blurred the Heath into nothingness—save where a single tree stood outlined against the gray sky, each black twig legible, one solitary, ghostly tree at a time. Corot painted mists like these, I've read, then stopped when they cleared. "Everything can be seen now. And so there's nothing to see."

By this time the Heath boasted no highwaymen, gypsies, or nightingales. Constable had painted cows in the Vale of Health. Once the wolf and wild boar were hunted in its forest depths. Yet any afternoon before dusk, we could walk alone till we reached Ken Wood and, rising beyond it, the stately mansion built by Adam in George III's reign. We could go inside and gaze at the Vermeer over the grand piano. Or wander down the hill to Wentworth Place, just off the Heath, and spend an hour in Keats's house. Or sit on Henry James's favorite bench that he had photographed to immortalize it. No village green in the world offered more except a band concert.

Lytton Strachey wrote in sylvan utterance to Virginia Woolf: "There are moments—on the Heath, of course—when I seem to myself to see life steadily and see it whole. . . ."

The more to see life steadily and whole, we stopped sooner or later in our appointed rounds for half a bitter at a Hampstead pub. The choice was wide (more than six thousand pubs in Britain). There was the Spaniards Inn, alluring for its framed message over the fireplace that on an evening in May, 1819, John Keats had left a party of friends at the

Inn and gone outside to lie beneath a pine tree to hear a nightingale sing overhead, after which he wrote the "Ode to a Nightingale."

B. and I reverently lifted our glasses to drink to that extraordinary bird, which his friend Charles Brown said was singing its heart out in a *plum* tree, while under it Keats listened one May morning at Wentworth Place. We liked to sit under this same plum tree on visits to Keats's house, taking special satisfaction in the fact it was a *mulberry*. This was the nearest we came to listening to a nightingale.

There was Jack Straw's Castle, minus the company of Dick Turpin and the highwaymen. We spent an evening there in the company of Christopher, a tall, unassuming young gentleman studying for a career in the City, who lived next door to us in the Hotel Sandringham, a small residence hotel. Christopher was a great-grandson of Gladstone, a connection he dismissed as less than mentionable in these days—the Grand Old Man who had bored Victoria stiff.

"You must be a Liberal, in that case?" B. asked him.

"My parents are," Christopher said. "Family loyalty, don't you know. Moral principles and so forth. They come close to being the last Liberals in England, aside from the Manchester *Guardian*. As for me, good Lord no, I vote Labour."

Our regular pub was our local, the Coach and Horses, on nearby Heath Street among the wan tea cafés whose placard in the window announced the next Hampstead whist drive. There we were known, there we belonged, with Mrs. Ellen Turton, publican and barmaid, leaning over the bar to greet us, "What's yours, luv?"; her flaming red-haired daughter Gladys smiling a welcome, "Right you are, ducks"; her son Harry calling out, "Hello, dear, the usual this time?"

A coal fire burned in the fireplace. Over it an enormous

sign said COURAGE. It was a tiny place as pubs go, shining with gin bottles and pewter mugs, bright with jars of red roses. I admired the roses most of all—an England of red roses for courage, red geraniums for survival.

They questioned us, these friends: the unpublished poet, Ian, a roaring boy. The out-of-work actor, Cyril. The antique dealer with ivory Madonna figurines in his pocket. The stout wife, Molly, from the "Cresta," a Polish restaurant across the street. The kept girl, Gracie, nicely padded out and overblown, a tail tosser, considered at the pub a tearing beauty, though B. stayed impervious to her charm (I think). After returning to North Carolina I used to send nylon stockings to Gracie in the pages of the *New Yorker*, one stocking an issue. It was my CARE package to her. "Smashing!" she wrote. "Wizard!"

They were more aware of us, as Americans, than we of them. Considering the recent Yankee invasion, why not? American soldiers had been quartered with them a long, tense, intolerable while. At the Coach and Horses they aired their theories and opinions of us—that in the States we were ruled by women, which accounted for the randy behavior of American servicemen out of sight of the wife (Gracie's view). As a people, they agreed, we were oversexed and boisterous with some exceptions.

And I would answer mildly, "You bet we are."

"We prefer your quiet Americans," Molly said, "over your more flamboyant ones. Hopefully," she added with a gracious nod, "you take my meaning, no slight intended, I'm sure."

Of a Saturday night, when the customers played darts and Gladys banged the piano for the group singing, oh boy, you should have heard the quiet English then.

They respected our ability to survive in the States without pubs, prostrated and congealed in turn by the weather, threatened by gangsters who had taken the place of the red Indians in stalking us and shooting us down in broad daylight.

"Do they come at you with tommy guns?" a patron asked, eager for an eyewitness report of the massacre.

The widow Turton had a niece by marriage living in Arkansas. "Would that be very near to you, luv?" she asked. "My, my, I do trust not, it does sound too terrifying, all those cyclones and all."

We told them what we could to make America suitably sensational. But we were soon abashed and silenced. No tall tale could match their casual accounts of life in London during the blitz to make the mind reel and the spine quiver. Everyone had his war story of personal survival, valor under fire, which he told modestly with no credit due to himself. The Germans had missed him. It was astonishing but accidental of a morning to wake up alive amid the death of so many.

A man had to choose on what terms he would meet the skyful of bombs. Though he expected to die, there was a limit to the concessions he would make. The Underground Station at Hampstead, the deepest in London, was always available as a bomb shelter. Some tried sleeping there and gave it up, preferring to live or die in the ferocious racket and burning above ground, with a little fresh air and privacy. Mr. Tilley built a wire mesh cage in his living room, into which he and his family crawled at night, safe from splinters of glass when the windows burst into fragments. Others dragged in sandbags, or stowed the children under the bed. "A bad show, that," was the worst they had to say of it. "Not to worry. We came through."

Freddie Baker, a Hampstead man, took his girl Kitty on Sunday all the way to the Anchor Inn in Bankside. He did so to leave more room in Hampstead for the Anchor regulars (hard beset by Bankside bombings) to spend Sunday on the Heath with a peaceful pint afterward at the Coach and Horses. Freddie's war experiences consisted in having been bombed twice, both times with a beer mug in hand at a London pub.

"A bleedin' hero, that's what I was," said Freddie.

"Mind your language," said Kitty.

VII

Even at the British Museum, the story went, during the air raids the readers disdained to take fright or cover. They removed their glasses and sat staring ahead, glasses in hand. When the All Clear sounded, they resumed reading. (The Museum suffered a direct hit one night and grave damage, 200,000 volumes lost but no readers. They had gone home to read.) Whether this story of the composure of scholars at bay was apocryphal or not, it fitted, consistent with the British character. They didn't scare. They had the temperament for survival without theatrics.

B. and I worked there daily, with a season pass issued to 393 of us scholars permitted to use the Reading Room and warned to mind our wallets since the Museum was full of thieves. Nothing was said of guarding other valuables—our fund of knowledge, our store of golden learning. I was present under false pretenses, as no doubt in his time was Karl Marx. Whatever good or ill Marx was up to, I wrote light verse, with books piled high around me as a ruse and a barricade.

A book I came across and kept on my desk like an amulet had the inspiring title *Helen Bevington, A True Story*. I coveted and seriously considered stealing it from the Museum when I could find no copy in a London bookshop. Printed in 1868, the work of an unidentified E.E. (clearly female, virgin-minded), it was a dreadful novel set in the eighteenth century, pure sentimental, stilted drivel, written in platitudes like these: "A Christian woman's sway is of untold worth."

"Time," it said, "the greatest healer of man's woes, brought health and joy to Helen Bevington, and she consented to become the wife of Stewart Fortescue." It provided genteel companionship but also a stern reminder to try to be literate.

B. was deep in research on a book about the Stephen family and its most celebrated member, Virginia Woolf, daughter of Leslie Stephen. We had come too late to meet Mrs. Woolf, who died a suicide by drowning in 1941, though before her death she had corresponded with B. about the history of her family.

Her sister Vanessa Bell, whom we knew and loved, gave every encouragement, being confirmed in the opinion that ancestry is all-important. To amount to anything one had to be born well, of exceptional parents and good family, preferably a family named Stephen. To be artistic, intellectual, or even interesting, one's forefathers must have handed down the heritage. Vanessa Bell required a stately family tree of any who pleased her (a condition she apparently waived for Americans). Her taste was selective and severe, and if on this point she seemed obstinate she had reason to be: her family had been of the intellectual aristocracy in England since the eighteenth century.

A claim to superior birth may be natural in a country that has produced so many great families and civilized minds. I remember when I met Mary Moorman, the delightful biographer of Wordsworth and wife of a bishop, she introduced herself by saying, "I am Trevelyan's daughter," not bothering to distinguish among the eminent Trevelyans or mention her father's first name. (She refrained from adding, "I am the granddaughter of Mrs. Humphry Ward.") It wasn't snobbery but caste, simple identification of one's privileged station in life. I could imagine the effect had I answered her, "And I am Charley Smith's girl."

It exasperated B. that I could never keep the generations of the Stephen family straight. Too many of them were named James (the Trevelyans were all George). He would run through the succession time and again.

"Let's start with James Stephen, Master in Chancery, M.P., born in 1758. He was son of James Stephen who wrote on imprisonment for debt, who was son of James Stephen of Aberdeenshire, who was son of James Stephen of Ardenbraught. . . . Are you with me? O.K., this James Stephen was father of Sir James Stephen, who was father of Sir James Fitzjames Stephen, who was father of James Kenneth Stephen and brother of Sir Leslie Stephen—"

"The friend of Wilberforce!" I cried triumphantly.

"Who was?"

"James Stephen!"

"Which James Stephen?"

"I don't know."

"You're absolutely hopeless," said B.

But one of them was the friend of Wilberforce, who was the friend of God and the friend of Man. It said so on the tomb we visited in the churchyard at Stoke Newington, scraping off the green moss from the huge stone box containing James Stephen to read his epitaph. Wilberforce, his brother-in-law, had promised that at death their ashes would be mingled in the same grave. Through a miscalculation it hadn't come about. Wilberforce went to Westminster Abbey instead. The two friends had been members of what Sydney Smith in derision called the Clapham Sect, who lived on

Clapham Common and fought with Evangelical zeal to abolish slavery in British colonies throughout the world.

Endearingly, this James Stephen had written a memoir (B. later edited and published it), in which he confessed in a steady flowing hand the rash misdemeanors and follies of his youth. The main one, described in total recall, was to father an illegitimate son, for which God and a compassionate Providence forgave him and led him to holier works. The son William grew up to be Vicar of Bledlow, Bucks.

In the midst of this sexual episode, a prolonged tale of delirious seduction—how he had lusted after Maria while remaining loyally in love with Nancy, thus proving to himself that a man can love two women at the same time—James Stephen paused one day and laid down his pen in mid-sentence. He had got through the first twenty-five years of his sinful life and already filled two stout volumes equipped with brass locks. As Spenser said in the *Faerie Queene*, "An huge heap of singulfs did oppress his struggling soul."

An amorous man, a Stephen and a self-revealer, he had lingered with gusto over this picture of wicked desire, remorse, and terror. "We were both undone," he wrote. Once a black cat got into the bedroom which he mistook for the Devil come to claim his own. After abandoning the unfortunate Maria and electing to marry Nancy and let her rear his bastard child (driving both women to the verge of suicide), even then he happened upon a Mrs. B., mistress of a Duke, and without ado succumbed once more. Only his second wife, Wilberforce's sister, managed years later to tame him. "O, she was the friend of my soul. She told me frankly all my faults."

It reads like a Gothic novel, an unfinished thriller of only 612 pages. Daunted perhaps by the length of a life yet to unravel, James Stephen broke off one day without a period to his sentence, rose from his desk, and closed the book. The memoir meant for the use of his children after his death, to tell them the man he was, had made its point: God had let him off. A merciful God of whom he now had proof wanted his soul saved, and God had saved him.

I think kindly of that uncompleted sentence. The publishers did not. Though B. explained, pleaded, raged through galley and page proof, all the instincts of the publishing world were against ending a book without a period. When the *Memoirs of James Stephen* appeared in print, a full stop had been added, a little black dot to say finis.

Our first weekend tour in the Anglia, in October, was to Fordingbridge, Hampshire, to visit one of the last remaining Stephens. This was Miss Dorothea. My soul and body! (as my mother used to say in wonder or alarm) what a woman. As an example of English durability and tough-mindedness, she bedazzled. When I saw how cunningly she had outwitted age at seventy-eight, I felt my life about to be extended. She didn't begin to creak. The thing to do was to study her method.

The youngest of ten children of James Fitzjames Stephen, a High Court judge, she was first cousin to Virginia and Vanessa. They played together as children in London in Victoria's reign. Yet later when B. told Vanessa Bell of having met Dorothea, her bored reply was, "Is that old girl still alive?"

Their adult worlds never touched—Vanessa a member of the freethinking Bloomsbury Group, Dorothea a loyal descendant of the Clapham Sect. Vanessa was a modern artist who, wrote Virginia Woolf, "looked on nakedness with a brush in her hand" and painted a thousand uninhibited pictures. Dorothea engaged wholly in good works, befriending the poor and relieving the distressed. She was a living, breathing Moral Code.

"But," she said, "my own father became a deliberate sceptic. Uncle Leslie was an agnostic to the day he died. Both abandoned all belief in Christianity, repelled by those who professed it."

Their views were not Dorothea's. With her the God of the Stephens did not perish. Like her antecedent James Stephen who created the family scandal, she gave a benevolent Almighty full credit for making her what she was—undefeatable and undefeated. Vanessa, more independent and less grateful, merely recognized the advantage of being a Stephen to start with.

I'm sorry Dorothea never married, the waste of a good woman, though it would have taken a strong, pious man to steer her. So much virginity had made her combustible. She exploded when she talked. She sat with a mouthful of opinions, red cheeks puffed with them, lips tight shut, till at last the words burst like firecrackers. For many years, I felt sure, no man had tried to quench her.

For example she had, in July, celebrated her great-great-grandfather's 293rd birthday (that would be the James Stephen imprisoned for debt). What does one make of a Stephen so much a Stephen as that?

"Well then!" she said, detonating. "How will our horrendous current problems and our solutions to them look in another 293 years?"

"I find I like meeting you," she said, and gave us her diary to read. It began April Fool's Day, 1887. She called it "Wild Oats," the journal of a laconic young girl who included a recipe for sponge cake, the birthday of the Duke of Connaught, and now and then the desperate entry: "God save the Queen." When she made a social call, she wrote, "Arrived all right, as perhaps was natural." Her account in red ink of Jubilee Day, June 22, when in a majestic parade Victoria celebrated fifty years of a golden reign, began, "We had bacon for breakfast!!" It was clear Dorothea was no Virginia Woolf.

The livelier occasions, non-Anglican but instructive, were the visits to Vanessa Bell at Charleston, her home in Firle, Sussex. She invited us twice. Each time we went down by train to spend the day with her, her husband Clive Bell, and the artist Duncan Grant. Charleston was an ordinary farmhouse with shabby furniture and small rooms made exquisite by Vanessa's and Duncan's paintings, whose work I couldn't tell apart. The three of them presented a perfect design for living, so neat that after a first view of it, on the trip back to London, I said to B., "Let's have one ourselves."

"Have what?" he said.

"A *ménage à trois*."

"Let's."

"Do you *mean* it?" I cried. "Here she is, lucky Vanessa Bell, surrounded by two brilliant men who love her. One paints pictures at her side, the other praises her art. They're devoted companions. They scout conventional morals. It's a sensible plan and it works—three intelligent people living happily as one."

"Impressive," said B.

"What do you say?"

"Certainly."

"That's my love. I hoped you would."

"By all means!" said B. "Where do you think we can find a desirable young woman to come and live with us?"

They offered martinis before lunch and the hospitality of amusing gossip, mostly scandalous. Clive Bell was a ginger-haired, partly bald, large, gleeful man with a pink face and high spirits, who knew everybody of note in the art and literary world and with no show of malice told an ornamented all. He talked equally well of shooting partridges.

Duncan Grant, small and dark, so handsome one imagined how lovely he had been as a youth—and how many had loved him—spun out a racy tale, indiscreet with a guileless air.

And Vanessa listened, her smile wry and mocking, or she looked away withdrawn, not listening. Silence became her. She was silent by choice, crouched low in her armchair, smoking constantly, hearing or not hearing. She had been very beautiful, tall and blue-eyed like Athene, but the fact no longer concerned her. Clive remarked that his wife had a will of iron. Virginia Woolf wrote in her *Diary:* "I always measure myself against her and find her much the largest, most humane of the two of us."

Clive leaned toward me when a sudden thought struck him. "Have you met Tom Eliot yet?" Without waiting to find out, "There's a poet you must meet," he said, "bit aloof, prim sort really for an American, but we're quite fond of him. I *do* think you ought to know Tom Eliot. Nessa!" he called to his wife, who was staring into space fathoms deep, detached from the talk around her, "don't you agree she ought definitely to meet Tom?"

"Tom who?" asked Mrs. Bell in her faint, scornful voice.

By chance, later in the spring Alan Pryce-Jones, editor of the *Times Literary Supplement,* took us to lunch at the Savoy and made the same suggestion.

"Wouldn't you like to meet a poet?" he inquired.

Since Alan spoke with a clipped Oxford accent and we were absorbed anyway in eating the hard-boiled seagull's eggs (costly enough to swell a gull with pride) he had ordered for our lunch, I misunderstood the question. "Rabbit," I thought he said. "Wouldn't you like to meet a rabbit?"

Like Clive, Alan knew everybody of note, including Nancy Mitford. When I hesitated, wondering how to accept this kind invitation, Alan withdrew it.

"No," he said, "I don't suppose you would. There's T. S. Eliot, charming man, I'm devoted to him, though he does have a prankish sense of humor. He told me I was the model for that idiot Alex in *The Cocktail Party*."

By this I knew Alan referred to poets, but he never showed us one. We had to see Mr. Eliot (prim in profile, not actively prankish) for ourselves by sitting behind him one night at a London performance of *The Family Reunion*. After the final curtain, he twisted around and asked B. how to get out of the theater. Aware that here at last was a poet who had lost his direction, B. gladly told Mr. Eliot the way that he must go.

Concerning the members of her family, Vanessa Bell was wordless, nearly so. She went to find a book of photographs of the Stephens taken by her great-aunt Julia Cameron, then mocked their Victorian quaintness.

"See how absurd we were," she said, "the Burne-Jones poses"— her bearded father Leslie Stephen, her lovely pre-Raphaelite mother, Virginia and Vanessa as little girls, their brothers Adrian and Thoby.

She brought out and silently handed us to read (not mocking them) letters and poems written by her son, Julian Bell, killed in the Spanish Civil War in July, 1937. Vanessa, a pacifist, had bitterly opposed his going. She couldn't stop him, but because he adored her he had become an ambulance driver instead of a member of the International Brigade— to no avail. He died anyway and died in vain. What had she left? A few letters, a few conventional nature poems about the "pale, ghostly woodcock" and the marsh birds.

Vanessa could not have written her life story, lacking the words (oddly, she belonged for thirty years to the Memoir

Club that met in Bloomsbury to read their memoirs aloud). But this death, like Virginia's suicide, must have turned her spirit toward the dark.

"Julian was a poet," she said, as if that was explanation enough.

Abruptly she changed the subject and questioned me. "What did your boys call you as children? Mama, did they say? Not Mum, I hope."

"Helen, mostly."

The answer pleased her. Among her many acts of revolt against Victorian propriety, she had required her three children to call her Nessa.

"And did you spank them?" she asked. "I never raised a hand against mine. I didn't believe in corporal punishment."

"I did," I said.

As proof of friendship, she gave us the Mausoleum Book to carry off to London and read at leisure—one more family diary, written by that voluminous author Leslie Stephen. Vanessa had named it jeeringly the Mausoleum Book (still in manuscript, unpublished), one more unfinished journal of the confessional Stephens. The habit ran like a flame through the family, to live with pen in hand, set down ideas, sponsor causes, invent plots, keep diaries, write tirelessly about themselves. To me this journal is the most engrossing of the lot.

Professional writer though he was, like his grandfather (the amorous James) Sir Leslie got snared in acute problems of recall, unable to extricate himself. A week after the death in 1895 of his beloved second wife, the former Mrs. Duckworth, he sat down to tell the history of their love, their blissful married life. It was a compulsive attempt to ease his racking grief and give his four children a picture of their mother, whose beauty was legendary.

"I wish to write mainly about your mother," he began.

"But I find in order to speak intelligibly it will be best to begin by saying something about myself."

There was the pitfall! Like a true memoirist he fell head-long into it to become the central dramatic character. For Leslie Stephen the tumble was predictable, so orderly was his mind as maker of the *Dictionary of National Biography,* so rectilinear, given to exact recording and meticulous out-line. In no time he found himself back in the days of his *first* marriage to Thackeray's daughter Minny twenty-eight years before, then back to the period when as an awkward young man out of Cambridge he had met and with methodic propriety courted the younger Miss Thackeray.

It was comical to watch his plight. This wasn't the love affair, the ideal union, he had meant to describe. How in the world had he got himself involved in the pursuit of *Minny?* For page after page, a thorough and conscientious reporter, he strove to whip the past into shape and dispose of life with Minny (who fell dead on his forty-third birthday) that he might dwell on his present inconsolable loss.

Yet by the time he had advanced belatedly to his starting place, much of the anguish had been dispelled. His account of Julia dwindled away, incomplete, untold. Soon he was listing the deaths of friends falling fast around him. Soon he was a feeble, deaf old man carrying an ear trumpet. He broke off on a note of self-pity to his children: "It comforts me to think that you are all so fond of each other that when I am gone you will be the better able to do without me." It had become a mausoleum book indeed. He had embalmed himself.

Nor did Leslie Stephen dredge up any noteworthy sins or peccadilloes along the way. While admitting his faults, which were maddening, he hadn't tried to correct them—a husband who (both times) felt unworthy yet acted the tyrant, wor-shipped yet was unkind. The unalterable ego proved too strong. It diminished him as a man. He was a sulker, a pouter, a wearing husband, a blind father. Wanting intensely to be loved (sometimes a sin in itself), he hurt those around him by an uncontrollable, imperious self-love. His children could only join forces against him and shut him out. Was it courage or blindness that drove him to write this damaging evidence of what was, for him, a happy marriage?

His deep depressions, inherited by Virginia, she attributed to the black blood of the Stephens. Unlike his erring grandfather, Leslie Stephen had no concern to demonstrate the will of God in saving his soul. It was appallingly clear his soul was not saved.

I found it a moving confession, in the end melancholy—a lesson in prolixity and how not to mastermind a household or write an autobiography. Unfinished confessions ran in the family. Virginia Woolf too laid down her diary one day to walk beside the river and never return.

". . . must cook dinner," she broke off. "Haddock and sausage meat. I think it is true that one gains a certain hold on sausage and haddock by writing them down."

Lytton Strachey's sisters, like Dorothea and Vanessa, made me suspect there must be virtue in this idea of being born well, at least if one wanted to survive into indomitable old age with the mind intact. Pernel, Philippa, and Marjorie Strachey had neither lovers nor piety but talents of another sort. They survived in this man's world as bold, dedicated feminists. They held advanced opinions on the woman question. And they held them long.

In his researches B. had no urge to take on that eccentric family. Yet during the year in England we went a number of times to tea at 51 Gordon Square because they invited us. The visits required some recuperation afterward.

I sat in the armchair under Lytton's drooping, disjointed,

languid portrait and rejoiced in his strong-minded sisters, the picture of vigor as he was of debility. It was tempting to think something original must have happened in the producing of this family of thirteen children, all feminist.

Pernel, known as "The Streak," now retired as Principal of Newnham College, University of Cambridge (so thin a streak, so extended in length she reminded one of a "not too French French bean"), had a daring mind and no doubt could do anything a man could do except start a war. For years Marjorie, the plainest, had kept a dame school at 51 Gordon Square for the little Bloomsberries, children of the Group. Whatever heresies she taught them, the main one (she told me) was adherence to woman's rights, though it was Philippa who became the embattled leader in that movement.

Philippa or Pippa (her mother doted on Browning) was a caution, a formidably emancipated woman of the kind one would have thought till lately as extinct as the buggy whip, with a shock of bobbed iron-gray hair that bristled like her. It stood out from her head like wires, expressing her militant convictions. She was not, in Browning's phrase, a "martyr to mild enthusiasm." She was the unsinkable one, the last of the Stracheys to survive.

Equality for women—did Philippa actually believe it could be won? Like the movers for Women's Liberation today, she did, she did. Echoing Margaret Fuller, who said "Men disappoint me so," she asserted our god-given rights to equality with men while stoutly maintaining our superiority as women. Her lofty sense of womanhood seemed at first innocent if overwrought, a banner with a strange device, but soon it became a club to beat one into submission and respect. A man-queller. My single desire was to bask in her esteem by hiding the revelation of my man-loving and enslaved self.

We talked over tea of Woman's Rights, what else? Philippa spoke in a penetrating voice as President of the Feminist Society in England. She had gathered a library of books concerning women of heroic resolve who distinguished themselves as pirates, spies, sea captains, suffragettes, heads of state. Assuming me to be an active supporter of the cause, she tended to ignore B. as belonging to an uninteresting sex. He in turn betrayed no domination of the male, especially since no way occurred to him to do so.

I tried to win her applause by telling her that, like the American pioneer Lucy Stone, I had kept my own name after marriage. This gesture impressed Philippa, a protest against loss of identity and surrender of personality, till the obvious fact struck her that the plan of liberation had failed. She gave me a hard look. I hadn't gone on keeping it.

(Dylan Thomas might have had Philippa in mind when in 1932 he wrote in a letter to Trevor Hughes: "The women of the world, perpetually out of perspective, cry Focus, Focus. . . .")

Still, it wasn't till we were leaving, the first afternoon, that she found me out. While handing me my coat with an approving pat, "Tell me," she inquired, "have you any children?"

"Two sons," I said.

Philippa drew herself up as if I had slapped her. She stared dumbfounded, her face pink as a teacake. Her hair looked dumbfounded too. Then she delivered the reproof.

"*Why?*" she asked. "Why aren't they daughters?"

VIII

❯❯❯❯❯❯❯❯❯❯❯❯❯❯❯❯❮❮❮❮❮❮❮❮❮❮❮❮❮❮

It was nearly Christmas but we couldn't go home, not after only three months spent of a sabbatical year.

While we waited at midnight in London for a transatlantic call to go through to Philip in Exeter, the telephone rang. It was the London operator.

"I say, can you tell me which of the states New Hampshire is in?"

"New Hampshire *is* a state," B. replied.

Silence at the other end.

"I said New Hampshire *is* a state!" B. yelled into the phone. "Damn it, it's a New England STATE. You know, Maine, New Hampshire, Vermont—"

A longer silence followed. B. rattled the receiver in a fury. At last came the very British voice, cool and skeptical.

"Are you *sure?*"

We were leaving for Ireland (vacating our room while the Jørgensens' two children were home from school for the holidays), and to hear their voices we telephoned both boys. They would be together over Christmas with friends in Cambridge. They sounded loving, undisturbed by our absence, happy.

Next day we drove in the Anglia to Liverpool, arriving

late that afternoon in total dark and a dilly of a pea-soup fog. We weren't sure we were in Liverpool or still in the British Isles. It was as if, blindly following a diamond-studded line in the highway, we crossed a black cloud-smothered river, leaping from tiny glittering stone to stone and on to the next stone that might not be there. This antic behavior raised the hair on my head and curled it.

Once we nearly hit a road sign in the murk and B. got out to light a match and look. He lit several matches. "Do you know what that cursed sign says? It says *Lay-by!*"

"That's ungrammatical," I said.

"No, it's for lovers," B. said. "They put up signs."

We ended, by the grace of God and B.'s stubbornness, at the door of the Adelphi Hotel. Its lights winked feebly in the fog. There we stopped to gather courage before striking out for the miles of Liverpool docks and, somewhere among them, the night boat to take us over the Irish Sea to Dublin. We found a small table in the hotel lounge. The orchestra had launched into a brisk popular number, "The Third Man," and the room tinkled with teacups and pink-shaded lamps.

B. was drumming lightly on the tablecloth to the music, smiling into my eyes with relief at having saved our necks, when without warning I began to lose consciousness. The room blurred and swam. The rippling tune roared in my ears. In a panic, I rose from my chair but the nausea stopped me. It was safer to sit still.

"What's wrong, love?" B. asked, startled.

l shook my head.

"You look sick. You're trembling. Are you really *sick?*"

"Oh, yes. Oh God, yes! Definitely."

"Do you want some hot tea?"

"Yes, please."

"What is it? What's happened to you?"

"I'm homesick, that's all. I want to go home. It's ghastly. It's a greensickness."

"*Home*sick?"

"I think I'm going to die."

B. didn't laugh. He held both my hands tight in his own and kissed them. And the music played on.

Dublin had nothing less to offer in December than the color green—St. Stephen's Green, the emerald mailboxes, green moss on the trunks of trees. You would think the idea of green first came to mind in Ireland and never languished; they laid claim to it. I felt an odd sense of home. People on the street looked familiar, like someone I ought to recognize. I asked B. about this.

"It's the bartenders," he said. "You lived in New York where the bartenders were Irish. Everybody in Dublin looks like an Irish bartender."

"And the women?"

"They look like his sister."

We spent Christmas Day walking in the hills of County Wicklow, here a lough and there a demesne, seeing nobody. I'm wrong. That morning at Bray, twelve miles from Dublin, Father Christmas—a fat laughing fellow in red suit and white whiskers, surrounded by a mob of children—was playing on an accordion "It's a Long Way to Tipperary."

In the Wicklow hills was Glendalough, a wild lonely mountain glen bright with yellow gorse (Gogarty tells of a bird that knelt down and crossed itself at the sight of a gorse bush). A grim collection of ecclesiastical ruins were scattered there, the remains of a monastery founded by St. Kevin, who died in 618. I loved him for his patience. When St. Kevin lifted his hands suppliant in prayer, a blackbird lit on his upturned palm, built her nest, laid her eggs, hatched the eggs, fed the young brood, and taught the fledglings to fly.

At last they all flew away, after which St. Kevin lowered his hands. Of course the same story is told of Buddha, except that they were swallows nesting in his outstretched hands. And when they flew away, Buddha wept.

We returned for Christmas goose at the Standard Hotel, where we stayed in Dublin. That night we met two angry people sitting alone and apart in an empty lounge. So the day ended.

One was an Irish Lady Somebody, wearing a low-cut pink satin evening gown and a liberal collection of pearls and diamonds. You wouldn't mistake her for a lady (or for Yeats's friend Lady Gregory, either, who used to stay at the Standard). This one was old and ill-tempered, wealthy but with nowhere to go, titled but without friends—a cross old woman whom nobody loved. She kept her pride well honed by being rude to the waitress who brought the coffee.

"Americans," she said, looking peeved as we entered the lounge. It sounded like an insult. "Are you R.C.?"

"No," said B. Apparently he knew what R.C. meant. I didn't, but we sat down anyway.

"What state are you from?"

"North Carolina."

"I've traveled over the entire globe, including America," she said, her face wrinkled with years and disdain. "I know where North Carolina is, but I must say I have no wish to go there. It is north of Virginia."

"We call it south of back home," B. said lightly. "On the map it tends to appear just below Virginia."

"You are wrong," said Lady Somebody. "No one needs to tell me where Virginia is because I have *been* in Virginia. I have visited in Richmond, Virginia, which I believe entitles me to an opinion."

So we left it north of, her way.

After she had finished her coffee and sailed out of the

room like Juno and the Paycock, the only other occupant, slumped in a corner of the lounge with his back to us, rose and revealed his anguished face.

"How can you listen to a vicious old woman like that?" he asked. "Why do you let her treat you with contempt, with insolence, and say not a word to defend yourselves? She is evil. She despises you, you know, for being American and Protestant. In this country, you're an Irish Catholic or you're nothing."

"Poor old girl, I couldn't care less what she thinks," B. said.

"But you see? You needn't live in Dublin with her kind," the man said. "You are not like me. She has demanded that I be evicted from this hotel. She has threatened me. In her bigotry she would destroy me if she could. I am a Jew."

So was Joyce's Mr. Bloom a lonely Jew in Dublin, rejected and despised. But this man's hurt was infinitely worse. He was a Jew whose wife and daughter had died by hate in Belsen.

The loveliest sight in Dublin was the River Liffey that rose in the Wicklow hills and bisected the city. With her white swans and a Guinness barge floating side by side, at night the climbing moon of Yeats, she was Anna Livia Plurabelle herself, "All them liffeying waters of . . ."

"Mother of God!" said an Irishman standing beside us on O'Connell Bridge, "will you look at her?" It was here, he told us with pride, the Liffey ran red with blood for a week in the Easter Rising of 1916 when the fight with the British started in the General Post Office and the blood came pouring in a stream down O'Connell Street. He could lie in the telling if he pleased. I believed him. There was nothing to see now at the General Post Office except its Ionic portico with six fluted columns.

"One way I try to keep alive," B. said in my ear,

"is to arrive on the scene too late for a bloody insurrection."

Like the Irish Lady Somebody, Dubliners were careful to put a finger on you. They had a strong sense of God and demanded to know the state of your connection. You were challenged, identified, labeled on the spot by pubkeeper and cab driver alike. "Are you R.C.?" they asked. Are you one of us?

"Why do you ask?"

"Well now, some are, some aren't. There's no mistaking the two of you and that's a fact, is there now?"

I wasn't used to declaring my religion at the drop of a hat, or my feelings toward the English, the six Orange Counties, or the unspeakable Gaelic tongue.

They spoke the English tongue in Dublin, but their fists were up. In the Irish Free State, with the revolutionary leaders like Michael Collins dead and the battle over, why did the victors have such a sense of defeat in their victory? They fought on, belligerent, intensely nationalistic, for what they had bled so many centuries to get—and got.

At least St. Patrick's Cathedral was still Protestant, where Swift served as Dean for thirty-two miserable years and died a mad old man, buried in the nave next his beloved Stella. Down the south choir aisle of the Cathedral, I stopped to read an inscription on a family vault:

> As you are, so were wee:
> And as wee are so shall you be.

Where had I seen the words before? It came to me I was thinking again of Leopold Bloom. In *Ulysses* as Mr. Bloom walked in Glasnevin Cemetery, the Catholic burial ground where Daniel O'Connell the Liberator and Parnell lay buried, he reflected on mortality by echoing this epitaph:

"How many! All these here once walked Dublin. Faithful departed. As you are now so once were we."

Surely the lines had a common source as a graveyard

inscription. What would an Irishman like James Joyce be doing reading fate in the tombstones of St. Patrick's?

After the holidays, we settled into congenial family life with the Jørgensens, where during the winter in London whatever happened made the English seem more English, none the worse for that. And Jørgensen went on staging nightly his morality plays.

In America the Red hunt had begun. On January 21, Alger Hiss was found guilty by American courts and sentenced to five years in prison. For once in his life, Jørgensen was taken by surprise: no English court would have convicted a man on such questionable evidence given by a confessed perjurer and chronic liar. America was scared witless and hysterical. Already Senator Joe McCarthy had set out with a roar to prove the State Department infested with 284 card-carrying Communists and subversives, with Secretary of State Dean Acheson the reddest of the lot.

Unlike us, the English stayed unterrified. B. and I heard J. B. S. Haldane give a public lecture at University College, London, where Haldane spoke as an esteemed professor, well known though he was as a biochemist turned Communist, follower of the Party line, loyal supporter of Stalin's dictatorship. (A few years later, Herbert Read, a declared Anarchist, was knighted by the Queen.)

Haldane lectured on "Some Modern Views on Evolution," which conveyed to me no inflammatory ideas and resulted in no conversion. It's true he delivered a startling remark that stirred me, but what it had to do with evolution or Communism he didn't say.

"How do you know," asked J. B. S. Haldane, "that the planet Mars isn't carried around by an angel?"

In America, with the folly of McCarthyism and the hydrogen bomb, we were descending into depths ever blacker of the Atomic Age. On January 31, President Truman ordered work begun on the H Bomb, the thermonuclear superbomb one thousand times more destructive than before, the deadliest weapon so far known to man. Soon the first hydrogen bomb plant would rise near Ellenton, South Carolina, over the border from home. Einstein cautioned us again of the fatal consequences—the possible death of the planet.

Jørgensen, more irascible than ever, called it the Big Stick made ready to wield against Soviet Russia. "That does it!" he said, his voice shrill in anger. "Quite a shillelagh this time."

From the Visitors' Gallery of the House of Commons, we heard a spirited debate one afternoon on the "Married Women" bill. It sounded crucial to me, though even B., listening attentively, failed to grasp what the bill, identified as "Married Women (Restraint upon Anticipation)" was about or what if anything could be done about it.

"No, my love, it does not concern pregnancy," B. said to quiet my anxiety.

"Want to bet? There's an Anticipation Department at Selfridges."

"Good. But stop clamoring."

"Do they mean birth control, then?" I whispered.

"I don't think so."

"It can't be. That would mean restraint *before* anticipation. Oh B., what *are* they talking about?"

Nor did we learn from the Minister of Food, Mr. John Strachey, how much edible mutton tallow was going rancid in the United Kingdom. I grew the more impressed by Jørgensen's built-in ability to attend sessions of Parliament and sort out and absorb the news. I admired the grave decorum of the members, the way each Labourite and Conservative on entering or leaving the chamber bowed to the Chair, with nobody in it; the way, unlike our Congressmen, they abstained from reading newspapers or chewing gum. Mr. Churchill, however, sat and ate jujubes.

At the London Zoo, we saw a live English sparrow inside a lion's cage. The lion was fierce and awesome, pent up, snarling in fury, ready to destroy the world. Its tail moved like a whiplash. It gave a bellowing roar.

In a shaft of sunlight the appetizing little sparrow picked about with a busy air, uncramped by its quarters, inattentive to the enemy slavering overhead. Being a seed eater, maybe it hadn't learned what a meat eater eats. Maybe it was deaf. Maybe it was an unlicked, know-all bird, aware of being English, lacking the propriety to quail before immensities. Maybe it believed in peaceful coexistence with lions, a lover of world peace. Maybe it survived.

But Skelton's Philip Sparrow was eaten by a cat.

> For the soul of Philip Sparrow,
> That was late slain at Carrow . . .
> And for all sparrows' souls . . .
> *Pater noster qui*
> With an *Ave Mari*.

At the Freemasons Arms, Hampstead, they offered you beer and skittles. This game of ninepins, popular for six centuries but rarely played now in the pubs where it flourished, was meant for brawny men. A player hurled down the alley a flat oval piece of wood, the cheese, weighing ten pounds. In early times the Britons threw a sheep's joint instead.

The night we joined the game it was being played by three spry old men, straining and teetering as they sent the cheese rolling toward the nine wooden pins. Over our beer afterward, they gibed at the puny young fellows who preferred the silly game of darts. Too little skill these days, too little time.

As I listened I thought of the celebrated high-class whore of the late nineteenth century known as "Skittles" for her proficiency in the skittles alley (she cut a fine figure too on roller skates), a wanton beauty with bright hair, "Brave as a falcon and as merciless." The Prince of Wales attended her fashionable evening parties, and Gladstone once ventured to take tea with her. The poet Wilfred Scawen Blunt fell madly in love with Skittles, "A woman most complete in all her ways of loving." In scalding love poems he mourned a heart set asteam, calling himself at her feet, "Sad child of doubt and passionate desires."

As they used to say in Victoria's reign: "Life is not all beer and skittles." Or did they mean Skittles?

Since George Bernard Shaw still lived at Shaw's Corner, Ayot St. Lawrence, we drove out one Sunday to the tiny Hertfordshire village thirty miles from London to have a look at him. He died in that house in November of the same year, 1950, and we never caught a glimpse of his ancient, fragile self.

Yet in a sense we did. By peering through his gate, we made a close study of his garden, filled with rows and rows of brussels sprouts. (A visitor to literary shrines must be content.) What we beheld was not Shaw in person but what sustained and fed him and, so to speak, became the Inner Shaw.

Later I read that his ashes, mixed with his wife's and stirred with a kitchen spoon, were spread by spoonfuls over the garden.

At William Cowper's little house in Olney, Bucks., the trap door attracted us through which his three hares hopped into the parlor to keep the poet company. They trooped in at teatime, ears twitching, noses quivering, and romped on the carpet while he read his verses aloud. He never ate one.

Though all three were male, Cowper named them Puss, Tiny, and Bess. (When I put them in a verse, the *New Yorker* editors asked if I had invented these names. Would I call a male rabbit Bess?) Puss, a charmer, friendly as a cat to leap into his lap, died of old age at eleven years, eleven months. Cowper wrote his epitaph in Latin. Bess was gay and droll but died young. Tiny grew into a large, mean, surly, harebrained beast, quick to bite, undeserving the intimate acquaintance of a poet.

The marvel to me was the way a rabbit could move Cowper to poetry:

> A Turkey carpet was his lawn,
> Whereon he loved to bound,
> To skip and gambol like a fawn,
> And swing his rump around.

I met only one living poet, John Betjeman, at a poetry reading at Grosvenor House. He was a wayward fellow— though no more wayward as comics go than Falstaff or W. C. Fields—a natural funnyman terrified of extinction.

The small audience willingly caught his mood as cavorter, his zany humor and prancing rhymes, the comedy of his personal fripperies, such as his habit of falling in love with big athletic girls with sturdy legs who beat him at tennis:

> Fair tigress of the tennis courts,
> So short in sleeve and strong in shorts

That was fine. Then sobriety broke in, and with dolor and grief in a discomfiting shift Mr. Betjeman's round face grew dark with horror. Before our bewildered eyes, he lay moribund, his mind unhinged, his thoughts turmoiled by death as he plucked at the sheets in a hospital room, dying abandoned and alone:

> And say shall I groan in dying
> as I twist the sweaty sheet?

I liked him better when he was funny. Anybody can be afraid to die.

The village of Selborne, Hampshire, was obviously the place to spend the rest of one's life. It seemed a pity we couldn't arrange to do so. Gilbert White found Selborne as suitable as Eden, complete with maypole on the village green, though the maypole like Eden had since disappeared. In his quiet house The Wakes he lived and died, first taking care to be born on the premises. There, since he had world enough and time, he was content to want no more.

Like Thoreau (and I wished I could say as much of myself), Mr. White took pleasure simply in the nature of a day, with its warblers and hedge sparrows. Still, I think he would have called Thoreau's two-year sojourn at Walden somewhat hasty, a mere overnight stay, a flying visit. Thoreau's journal too in fourteen volumes might have struck him as unmercifully long-winded. His own journal of twenty-five years was tidy and terse, limited to short entries: "Wheeled dung." "Blue stinking mist." "Large broods of long-tailed titmice." "Swifts squeak much." "Rooks live hard." "Curlews clamor." "Thistledown flies." No terrors were recorded, no mishap worse than the fact that the village idiot fell down a deep well twice in one day.

A man could live without makeshift or frayed edges in Selborne. So could a woman. I wished I might find the world unbeset, calm before my eyes as Mr. White did, along with the peace. But his world was not mine. Anyway our stopover was for the purpose admittedly brief.

IX

❦❦❦❦❦❦❦❦❦❦❦❦❦❦❦❦❦❦❦❦❦❦❦❦❦❦❦

The right way to cross the English Channel is from Dover to Calais, the shortest route to the Continent. Or we might have landed at Ostend or Boulogne or Dieppe. Instead we made the mistake of crossing to Dunkirk, of all ungodly places. On March first, after months of hoarding gas coupons, we set out on a two-month holiday in the Anglia. They had plenty of *l'essence* in France. It was snowing on the snowdrops as we left London, covering the crocuses in Hyde Park.

The night spent in Dunkirk was as close to intolerable, as desolate, as unhappy, as I care to spend. Should one be glad to have come no nearer to the terrors of war? Believe me, I was glad. But in a destroyed place the moment is less than fitting to thank one's stars and exult.

Snow fell as we left the channel boat and ice-filled Dunkirk harbor. In glacial dark we drove groping our way into an unlighted ghost town that had, it appeared, no people in it, or people hiding in their shuttered houses awaiting another bombardment or already dead. The skyline loomed jagged and slashed with the black silhouette of sharp projecting ruins.

Dunkirk had been all but annihilated, on fire and blazing,

during the week of the evacuation. A tall plume of smoke marked the city as German bombs fell on it, they say, every five minutes day and night. Again in 1944 it was nearly demolished, this time by Allied bombing. (Who *is* the enemy to those being bombed?)

By the time we found and registered at the Hotel Métropole—itself badly damaged, bleak and dimlit like a barracks, empty of patrons—I was ready to flee, thoroughly routed. Once we reached our bare little room, I began to weep. On the table was one frayed towel and a pile of neatly cut pieces of newspaper. On the wall a printed sign warned it was strictly forbidden to throw newspaper into the toilet. This was a nightmare by Kafka. It chattered my teeth. I implored B. to take us out of the lunacy of Dunkirk.

"Get the car," I said, "now, tonight, this minute! I don't want to stay here. Please hurry. Get the car and let's go, let's *go!*"

He wouldn't hear to it, of course. It was nearly midnight and snowing hard.

"We're together," he said. "What are you afraid of?"

"The ghosts of Dunkirk."

"But you don't believe in ghosts."

"I believe in fear," I said.

So we stuck it out sleepless till daylight, then on icy roads began to drive straight down the middle of France.

Spring arrived a little south of Paris, each day offering a few more apricot and plum trees in bloom. The white empty roads in the Loire valley became long avenues of plane trees. Magpies led the way. I learned at our breakneck speed of forty miles an hour what a good thing a *kilomètre* is. If we were *trente kilomètres* from Orléans, say, and like the Anglia dog-tired, panting to stop, I had but to multiply by .6 and, aha, we had eighteen miles to go. B. taught me that.

(Actually a kilometer is about ⅝ths of a mile, but B. knew I couldn't multiply fractions in my head.)

It was he as tour conductor who found us the best onion soup, at Cambrai, and the best champagne, at the *caves* at Épernay, where in deep labyrinthine cellars, fifteen miles of them hollowed out of the chalk hillsides beside the Marne, we walked among the twenty million bottles stored there of Möet et Chandon. This was spelunking on the heroic scale.

As we returned to the surface from a morning of lull and repose in these dark subterranean galleries, we were met by an official of the company, who invited us to drink a bottle of champagne with him. Perhaps he felt hospitable or dry before lunch. It was served in crystal saucers at a table covered with white linen, and I was moved by the gusto with which he sipped, the fervor with which he spoke.

"*La vie, Madame, Monsieur,*" he said gravely, lifting his glass.

"*La vie,*" we murmured.

Were he to be deprived of *le champagne mousseux*, nectar of the gods, that he drank every day of his life, he would deteriorate in body and mind. His flesh would fall into decay, his mind would fail. He would, in effect, die.

"*La mort, Madame, Monsieur,*" he said, lifting his glass.

"*La mort,*" we echoed.

Since there was a bit of the white sparkling wine left in the bottle, B. rose and proposed the last toast.

"*La vie et la mort,*" he said.

At Vichy we had vichyssoise, at Châteauneuf-du-Pape we had Châteauneuf-du-Pape. It was growing into a grand tour. I felt spared not to be traveling with Henry James, who wrote with fearful tedium of his tour of France, reminding his readers that any journey has its dull moments. With Henry James, yes. Dr. Johnson would have made a regrettable companion, who wrote of his French journey with the Thrales:

> À Amiens
> On n'a rien.

With a guidebook on my lap, I thought how times had improved:

> À Amiens
> On a Michelin.

The cathedrals were lively as a marketplace—Amiens, Rheims, Notre-Dame, Chartres—since this was a Holy Year. Within their flung-open welcoming doors we weren't ignored as unshriven tourists but greeted as pilgrims by other pilgrims, who silently gave us a pilgrim handshake, something like that exchanged between members of Phi Beta Kappa. We soon learned the trick of clasping hands and never let on.

Our destination was a seaside resort town near St. Tropez, not on the gray English Channel like Dunkirk but on the blue Mediterranean Sea, where all would be well on the Côte d'Azur et d'Or—sunny, warm, safe, happy. Its name was Hyères, about which Robert Louis Stevenson had written: "I was only happy once, that was at Hyères." It seemed as good a reason as any for going anywhere.

At Hyères, the pink almond trees blossomed, the grass was carpeted with gold *boutons d'or* and grape hyacinths. Palm, cork, eucalyptus trees lined the Avenue des Îles d'Or. Nuns passed riding bicycles. On the hillsides were green vineyards, groves of silver olive trees. The one version of the sky, repeated daily, agreed with Manet's—*"Le soleil est Dieu."* Beyond lay the blinding blue water of La Mer.

What was this talk of being *happy* at Hyères? How should one presume to be otherwise? Was this a place to weep or die, to complain of such beauty and well-being, such felicity? It would be an impudence to grieve, a morbidity, a base ingratitude.

In the mind were Stevenson's words. He had found happiness, the greatest in his life. He had lived at Hyères for eighteen months with his wife Fanny in a charming doll's house called La Solitude on the slope of a hill above the town, with a garden like a fairy tale (he said), "Angels, I know, frequent it," a view like a classical landscape.

Of course he ate ortolans, and I do not approve of eating little songbirds (buntings, larks, or thrushes). Of course Fanny had an evil temper, a barbarous woman, discontented, bossy, quarrelsome. Of course Stevenson nearly died one night of a hemorrhage so violent that, choked with blood and speechless, he scratched a farewell to Fanny: "Don't be frightened; if this is death it is an easy one." During that illness, before they fled Hyères when cholera broke out, he wrote his requiem:

> Home is the sailor, home from the sea,
> And the hunter home from the hill.

Yet the testimony was impressive. Years afterward, on three separate occasions, Stevenson repeated his claim to have found happiness: "How I wish I had died at Hyères, while all was well with me." "The bottom wish of my heart is that I had died at Hyères: the happy part of my life ended there." A third time, in 1888, he wrote, "Would God I had died at Hyères."

I might have gone on believing him. I might have conceded gladly he was right—it was possible even yet to be happy at Hyères. But that, I found, meant turning the eyes away. It meant denying the horror of the night in Dunkirk. Slowly the truth became too real, the proof too visible: this was only another Dunkirk, city of death. On August 15,

1944, the invasion of France by the Franco-American Army had begun at Hyères, launched from the small islands of Port-Cros and Levant off the coast, two months after the invasion of Normandy. Rabelais had loved them, "my islands of Hyères," heavy with the perfume of sweet herbs and flowers. The Allies arrived with one thousand ships. It was called the Second D Day.

Hyères became necessarily a target in the attack. During the troop landings more than four hundred villas on the stricken beach were destroyed. As one walked about now with eyes open, it was like touring a war area, forced to witness the scars and folly of the world. The town from end to end was pockmarked by machine-gun fire—the pink stucco houses on the Rue Paradis, the quaint Romanesque churches, flawed by the blemish of destruction, the scourge of war. During the bombardment a shell had fallen among the orange trees in the garden of La Solitude.

Except for the untouched, perpetual blue sea and the turquoise sky, nothing had been left whole. How could one look at Hyères and be happy?

After a few days we packed our bags and drove on down the coast, past Toulon, Bandol, la Ciotat. *Vive la paix,* but there was no peace. At noon we stopped for lunch at a tiny fishing village some fifteen miles this side of Marseilles. Its name was Cassis. Facing the seafront, where fishing nets were spread on the quay to dry, stood the modest Hotel Liautaud. They gave us food fit for the Worthies to eat: *omelette aux fines herbes,* artichoke vinaigrette just plucked from the garden, and the wine of Cassis. We laughed at having arrived by chance at the place itself. Nothing was amiss. Stevenson merely got the name wrong.

"I'm happy, are you?" I said to B.

For answer he jumped up to ask at the desk if they would

provide us with room and board at the Hotel Liautaud for, say, the rest of our lives?

Cassis-sur-mer has its casino nowadays with gambling, girls, and a night life to attract revelers from Marseilles. The old Cassis no longer exists, if it ever existed. At least it was well dreamed, once when it was full of sealight and water birds. *La maison reposait et le monde était calme.*

From our room beside the shimmering Mediterranean, after a late breakfast in bed of croissants and café au lait we stepped out to our balcony to scan the waterfront. Which of our friends had already settled at a table in the sun, drinking what nectar—morning coffee, a vermouth cassis, a pernod before lunch?

The Cornfords were young honeymooners from London, whom we loved on sight, on second sight as well. Cliff was in the Air Ministry, a cousin of the poet Cornford killed in the Spanish War. Kay, a slim little Irish girl, had married, she said, above herself and thanked God for that. After a month in Cassis, they went home to Frimley Green, Surrey, and had predictably, in the years to come, six children. And we visited them there and I heard a cuckoo in their garden.

Down at the waterfront, Cliff lifted his wine glass to squint through it at the cloudless sky. "Bevs," he would ask, "what does Mistral say about the weather?"

Mistral was a Provençal poet and a northerly wind. Each morning the newspaper reported without fail: *"Mistral modéré à assez fort."*

So we replied, "The wind is calm. The poet is *modéré à assez fort,"* which was true. B. and I had been reading him, a windy poet, definitely *du vent.*

"Good!" said Cliff. "Proper day for a picnic."

And so was yesterday. And so was tomorrow.

The hotel packed us a lunch of a loaf of French bread,

Camembert cheese, slivers of ham, two bottles of red wine, and a *pound* of butter. We went off to climb like goats the rocky spires surrounding Cassis, or in a boat to investigate like seagulls the *Calanques,* the rocky gorges and coves along the Mediterranean.

Terrified of heights, unlike the others I would get down and crawl on my belly up a steep slope that narrowed to perpendicular near the peak while the land fell away on all four sides. At the top we sat clinging like a perched village high above the sea. It was a mighty ascent for a pound of butter.

The Vitelleschis never joined these excursions because he had been badly wounded in World War II and limped along with a cane. Besides, they had too much flair to be scrambling about, too much dignity.

He was an Italian nobleman, Marchese Guido Nobili Vitelleschi, who lost his splendid courtesy and poise only at the mention of Mussolini. *"Cochon!"* he muttered and spat, or dropped a fierce Italian malediction, after which he apologized. "Forgive, Madame." Olga, the Marchesa, was French, a beguiling lady both elegant and vivacious near middle age, whose loyalty to her husband's country was so excessive she defended Italian food as superior to the best France had to offer. The reason was its infinite variety.

"Pourquoi pas? In Italy we have so many kinds of *pasta!"* she exclaimed.

They were aristocrats ruined by the war, who had come by bus from Rome for a brief economical holiday. In Rome they rented rooms in their palazzo to strangers, mostly Americans. Their attempts at English were fanciful, their manners exquisite.

We took the Vitelleschis several times in the Anglia to Marseilles, to eat bouillabaisse, to attend Mass at Notre-

Dame-de-la-Garde, a church high on a granite pinnacle above the city. From there, it seemed to me, one had a perfect panoramic view of how man had failed his surroundings. Beneath a magnificence of encircling mountains, beside a glitter of blue sea, sat the cheapest, most abject and squalid of cities, a sailors' port, tough, sinister, and badly war-damaged, all achieved by man's efforts—Marseilles.

One afternoon we went with them to a matinee at a music hall to hear Edith Piaf. We arrived in time for the turn that preceded hers, a performance by Fernand Sardou, who swished out onto the huge stage dressed half as a man in a tuxedo and half as a glamorous woman in a scarlet Spanish dress with flounces, her glossy black hair held with a comb at her neck. After a whirling, stamping dance, Sardou in a hot embrace began to make turbulent love to himself, with the male side of him caressing the aroused and amorous female side in increasingly indecent gestures, till one wondered honestly where the affair would end.

The Vitelleschis sat in their seats like stone carvings. Afterward they ignored the erotic exhibition, not shocked but dismissive. Neither by shrug nor raised eyebrow did they acknowledge vulgarity.

But Edith Piaf. She was an artist, a French artist, *inoubliable*. The Marchesa told me so, attempting a whispered translation of the songs at their most heartbroken. ("I had so much love for a man who had too little for me.") She needn't have tried, not that I caught the words. Like all Marseilles I mourned for the griefs of love—for Piaf the sparrow, the waif, alone on a bare stage in her short black dress, not chic, white-faced, hands tense, feet apart, wailing her moan for fifty lovers, all of whom had without ado abandoned her. She looked too frail for such incurable persistence, such lament, and so many desertions.

"Il fait bon t'aimer," she sobbed. What was good about it?

To a man they had stayed just long enough to rend her heart. Yet the audience fully suffered her woe, having been deceived often enough themselves. None knew the reason better: *"C'est d'la faute."* The fault is love.

With the end of the program, B. and I stood up automatically to await the opening chords of "God Save the King." It was curious: at Marseilles nobody sang the *Marseillaise.*

By Holy Week of Holy Year, in mid-April, we were back in the cathedrals (Italian this time) on the road home to England by way of the nightspots of Nice and Monte Carlo. If the spectacle in both holy and unholy interiors was idolatrous to onlookers like us, it was for a display of passion one could neither understand nor share.

At the Casino in Monte Carlo, bejeweled and rapacious old women in lavish evening gowns sat hunched over the tables, their hands extended like claws with blood-red nails, their faces avid with hunger for the spinning roulette wheel beside them. The impassive croupiers in black coats stood like officiating priests, while the prayerful women strained with supplication and litany toward the ever-turning wheel.

In Siena, Ferrara, Padua during Holy Week, old women in black shawls and black dresses prostrated themselves, lying full length in the aisle of the cathedral, their faces avid with hunger for the wooden cross they had received from a priest and laid beside them on the stone floor. Washing the relic with their tears, they caressed and kissed it, embraced it, moving a finger up and down, up and down the body of the crucified Christ.

On the Saturday before Easter, Venice held its observances with a different air, one of carnival with brasses. At five that afternoon I never felt more devout in my life, over a cup of espresso outside Florian's in the Piazza San Marco, with the municipal band playing music from *Parsifal* as if it were written for cymbals and trumpets. We were at home among the saints and hallows (Canaletto, Wagner, Goethe, Byron —had anyone in his life *not* visited the square of St. Mark's?). In and out of the glittering church of San Marco streamed the pilgrims, while above them the sunlit gold Byzantine mosaics gave blessing, the four colossal bronze horses at the portal shone with holiness.

The square was in uproar, a *hurluberlu* of laughing Venetians and flying pigeons—thousands of pigeons on parade or beating their wings overhead as if they ran the concession (as if their predecessors hadn't been eaten during World War II). To cap it all, like a sudden annunciation the Good Friday music crashed to a stop and high above us the great pealing bells of the Campanile took over, deafening, chiming what message?—not the death of God but the resurrection, *"He lives! He lives!"*—while down from the harbor came marching a smart file of American sailors in Navy whites from the battle cruiser the *Newport News*. It was the finale of a musical comedy turned sacred in tone. It was ear-splitting. It was wonderful. A fine noisy day for salvation.

Easter itself we spent with Catullus, on the all-but-island Sirmio of Lake Garda. Catullus (born in nearby Verona, Romeo and Juliet's town) owned a pretty villa there two thousand years ago in Roman times, before Christ was born or crucified. Unsuitable, to be sure, for Christian festival, Sirmio kept the same look probably that Catullus loved, his almost island, *Paene insularum, Sirmio,* extending two miles into a clear sapphire lake surrounded by snow-topped mountains and slopes of olive trees.

In a restaurant at the end of the peninsula, where we had Easter dinner of young spring lamb (emblem of both the Lamb of God and pagan sacrifice), we talked of Catullus and how many kisses he had given Lesbia. And how many curses when the anguished affair of her faithlessness and profligacy was over ("... convey a last compendious curse To her I loved").

"Do you know the number, love?" I asked. "How many kisses did he say they added up to?"

B. who kept a store of poetry ever handy in his head obligingly quoted a line from Coleridge's translation: "And when they to a million mount . . ." That was close enough.

Odi et amo, he said to Lesbia. A kiss and a curse. *Frater, ave atque vale,* to his dead brother. Catullus had taught me most of the Latin I knew.

"Come to think of it," said B., "how much more do you need?"

Having followed the spring down in March, in April we followed it up again, the razzle-dazzle route for sightseers.

In Strasbourg it was the season of the truffle and the pink cathedral. Daffodils bloomed beside Lake Lucerne, windmills beside the Zuyder Zee. From Haarlem to The Hague we were drowned in the perfume of the hyacinth fields. Delft had become a placid blue landscape by Vermeer, as if only such peace were worth preserving. Bruges was florid with the crimsons, greens, purples of Memling, so that in the museum you stared at the purity of his colors, matching them with the gardens outside. On the main streets from Luxembourg to Brussels smiled the burgeoning face of Rita Hayworth.

In England, on the first of May as on the first of March, it was *snowing*. At last I could recite Housman with conviction: "About the woodland I will go To see the cherry hung with snow." Then these white petals quickly melted into the white hawthorn on Hampstead Heath, the avenue of white chestnut trees in Regent's Park, a tremendous bowl of white lilacs at teatime at the Dorchester, and I suppose, had we looked for them, white lambs bouncing around in Sussex.

It was May. The annual Chelsea Flower Show settled any doubt. Admission: one pound. I had expected a garden party, not this Battersea Fun Fair, held in a big circus tent of riotous flower exhibits, muddy walks, unfashionable crowds, and ladies in freshly blooming hats, each a flower show herself. The British, at their best as birdwatchers, also seemed to prefer flowers to people. While the rain poured outside, they splashed about among the fuchsias, clawing their way to a front-row view of a clematis, stephanotis, or yellow laburnum, the strident female voices gloating in the ear. "Ehew, I *do* think that's the thing. Yes, quite, oh quite. Right! Super! Jolly good."

"How inadequate words are," said one of them with emotion and hurried on.

Yet like me they gave their hearts to the small, retiring plants in the rock gardens—the primulas, anemones, and red nicotiana.

"I *say*, that's a shy little saxifrage!"

"Even the lowliest flower is valiant, Mrs. Giliver, if it's treated to a bit of room."

"The trouble with a rockery, I always say, Mrs. Brewster, is getting hold of the rocks."

The Jørgensens, with love and regret, had given us up after two months and rented our room to other occupants. So we moved next door to the Hotel Sandringham where, in No. 12, high on the third floor, we had a sweeping view of London from Highgate to the dome of St. Paul's. We had a sink, a shilling meter for the gasfire, and a hob for the teapot.

"Aow, you're in the bridal suite," the chambermaid said.

Miss Grigsbee and her companion, Miss Bate, managed

this private residence hotel of seventeen rooms and two baths. They gave us breakfast and dinner in the basement dining room, at separate tables for two covered with red-checked cloths. Every resident but us had his own marmalade jar kept in the china cupboard for his exclusive use, and only we were served ice water for breakfast. We were the only Americans. In consequence, the reticent English, holding aloof from each other but regarding us as harmless and transitory, were not reticent. On the contrary. Unless we went out for the evening, we heard someone's life history any night after dinner.

It had the common theme of loss and loneliness. There was the colonel's lady, whose husband had shipped her home to be rid of her while he stayed in Egypt. She read Jung and studied Greek. Her psychiatrist said she had good intuitive feelings.

"Feelings? Whatever for?" she asked.

There was the retired naval commander, a bachelor with one lung and one interest left in life—birdwatching; the electrical engineer whose forte was high voltage, though his own voltage was low; and the thirtyish schoolmistress, snuffly with head colds, whom no man would ever rescue from teaching Latin. The blond young chap with a German accent, shunned by the others, took us aside several times to praise New Jersey, which he had visited for a stay of six months. After a while this eager travelogue sounded downright monotonous.

"Didn't you see anything but New Jersey while you were in America?" I asked.

"I was a P.O.W.," he said.

There was the middle-aged couple who occupied separate rooms but shared a table for meals, their knees necessarily touching, each reading his book in stony silence. There was the wife living apart from her husband, unable to marry the lover who visited her room every night till midnight (her room was next to ours, and they came hand in hand to explain their hopeless predicament); the old couple from Yorkshire waiting months for their only daughter to die of terminal cancer in a London hospital.

The pattern was too drab, the emptiness too neat. I wondered where B. and I fitted in.

Even Miss Grigsbee and Miss Bate had, it seemed, some kind of agonizing relationship. We didn't learn much about it because Miss Bate stayed in the kitchen to do the cooking and Miss Grigsbee, stout and tweedy, a gabby woman, talked too loud and interminably under B.'s stoic gaze for him to bear up for long. One night in the lounge after dinner he rose to his feet in the midst of her recitation, just as she approached the promising part:

"Early on, Miss Bate and I found each other. We were mutually attracted, don't you see, and anyway the loneliness gets on you if you go it alone, so after my father died (he owned a small but select hotel of twenty rooms in Wiltshire which I had the entire management of singlehanded when he became crippled with rheumatism and quite helpless and my poor mother dead these many years), well, we decided to turn to, Miss Bate and I, don't you see, being mutually attracted as it were, and make a team of it . . ."

"Please excuse me," B. said. "I'm going to my room and curl up with a Trollope."

"Not very funny," I said, after pumping Miss Grigsbee's hand and following him out the door. "It was a corny exit, if you ask me. Besides, who's the bloody trollop?"

X

>>>>>>>>>>>>>>>><<<<<<<<<<<<<<<<

On the *Queen Mary* bound for America in June, I lay in my deckchair beside B. and, while he slept, thought of the sights worth returning to England for:

The golden beeches of Buckinghamshire
A glass of Devon cider
Winchester Cathedral with Jane Austen buried on the north aisle, Isaak Walton on the south
Mousehole, a village in Cornwall, with its Mousehole Male Voice Choir (not mice but men)
A swan on her nest in a Cotswold pond—a nest as big as a man would make if he lived like a bird or, like Zeus, became one.

Our cabin was perfumed with red roses from the pub. An armload of them had been delivered to the boat at Southampton with a card attached, "Fraternally yours, your loving friends at the Pub, the Coach and Horses."

With a painful wrench we had sold the little Anglia for five pounds more than we paid for it. We were the losers: like the Aga Khan it was worth its weight in gold. Now we came seaward home to our other possessions.

David at Harvard, distracted by a love affair and final examinations, took what time he could spare to welcome us. In Boston the Houghton Mifflin Company gave me a copy of my second book of verse, just published, titled for no good reason *Nineteen Million Elephants*. (In the *Origin of Species,* Darwin defined survival by the example of a pair of slow-breeding elephants, estimating that after 740 to 750 years, if none of the usual disasters occurred that overtake man and beast, there would be nineteen million elephants alive descended from the first pair.) All those smiling baby elephants gamboling over the cover made it look like a juvenile, an imitation *Babar*. Nobody got the title straight or saw its concern with survival. *Nine Pink Elephants* was as close as most readers came, though whatever the number the elephants loomed up pink. The customer is always right. Still, naming a book is trickier than naming a child, since you wouldn't saddle a newborn baby with a title nobody had used before.

From Cambridge the three of us drove to Exeter for Philip's graduation. He had received a scholarship to Harvard for next year. As David wrote us in England, "Thank God! he won't have to join the Navy!" At a garden party given by Mr. Saltonstall, headmaster at Exeter, to crowds of beaming and gratified parents, a stranger came up and inspected my face. "Pardon me," she said, "but I know who you are. I recognized you across the lawn. You're the mother of Bevingtons."

On the boat coming home, another lady, a spinster, had said, "How tragic for you to have borne sons. In a war-mad world like ours, sons only grow up to be cannon fodder."

Two weeks later, June 25, the next war began. Communist troops in a sudden attack invaded South Korea across the 38th parallel. Within two days President Truman replied with a threat of immediate military action. Korea became the new battleground to prevent World War III (which on the contrary we appeared to be fast bringing about), as Spain had been to prevent World War II. Scarcely five years after V-J Day we were at it again, fighting Communists instead of Nazis. To meet Soviet aggression, we risked a full-scale nuclear war, the annihilation of mankind, and kingdom come. As Jørgensen had predicted, we were at it again.

Few Americans knew enough geography for these wars or where Korea was—a small peninsula somewhere in Asia—or what we were fighting for. Most of us still wonder. With a dazed sense of repetition, we faced another enemy, another world crisis, enough to terrorize the gods, who would have to forgive the impertinence.

A few days later, David, a midshipman in his second year, was off to Pensacola and a naval cruise simulating battle conditions, being taught amphibious warfare against almost certain need.

"We're pretty upset down here over Korea," he wrote. "A long fighting war seems the only possibility."

Who could guess its duration or the outcome? Month by month things merely looked worse. When the Chinese Communists brought in their armies to defend the North, we were in grave danger of having to fight both China and Russia. It was the beginning of another botched decade. And my sons were now young men.

Yet as a family we went on surviving into the 1950's, as if there were peace left on earth. *As if.* B. and I refused to dig a bomb shelter in the backyard, though many of our friends, faced with the unsettling threat of extinction, acquired one as part of nature's plan—a simple hole in the ground or burrow furnished with bottled water, canned goods, and whatever else you deemed appropriate to preserve life. It was the latest thing in living quarters, a new kind of storm cellar for a new kind of cyclone. In case of attack the alternative would be to dive under the sofa, a lot less trouble, B. said, and equally effective.

People feared the mushroom cloud of death from the sky,

feared radioactive fallout, feared the possibility that the earth might shift on its axis or that a chain reaction might destroy the planet. Worst of all, in America we feared each other. Anyone during the war years might be hunted out and accused of disloyalty if he engaged in some un-American activity like joining a peace group or subscribing to the *Nation.* Only the foolhardy declared themselves openly in favor of peace or the brotherhood of man. To work for peace labeled one a left-wing radical, since such groups were said to be Communist controlled. We suspected spies and agitators everywhere. The innocent were found guilty by association. There was something too called "creeping socialism" that menaced the unwary.

Already many universities (like the University of North Carolina) required its faculty to sign loyalty oaths, sign or resign, and we awaited our turn at Duke. Fortunately it never came; we didn't have to swear *on oath* a love for our country. I could not imagine myself knuckling under like that. Certainly I knew B. would not submit.

When in October 1952 the loyalty of our closest friend, Donald Flanders, was questioned, B. flew out to Chicago to testify in the investigation. I was asked to inform by letter for or against him to aid the inquiry. Moll (his nickname, from Defoe's Moll) had been a mathematician with the group at Los Alamos that created and set off the first atomic bomb. Now at work at the Argonne Laboratory, he was accused of being a security risk and brought before the Personnel Security Board of the Atomic Energy Commission, suspected for one thing of guilt by association for being— let's see—the brother-in-law of the sister-in-law of Alger Hiss's wife. For another "item of derogatory information," Moll's daughter Ellen, a student at the University of Chicago, was said to have supported Henry Wallace in his campaign for president (though she changed her mind before the election and failed to vote for him).

After the ordeal of the hearings, *two years* passed before the board "cleared" him of any subversion. But the humiliation of facing such charges, the questioning, the doubts cast upon his character, his integrity and that of his wife and family, were shameful experiences from which he never fully recovered. Moll's innocence was beyond question. "His honesty is of the ultimate sort," I remember writing in his defense, "like Dr. Johnson's who spoke truth as if on oath." He kept his honor intact because he knew what honor is. Nobody could be more loyal than that.

Like Oppenheimer (whose security clearance was denied because of "proof of fundamental defects in his character"), he was repaid by his country in tragic coin, a victim of our national witch hunt, our Red scare and fierce hysteria. That the hurt went unbearably deep Moll's suicide proved a few years later.

The Korean War lasted through three years of murderous fighting, several times on the brink of becoming World War III—as when General MacArthur tried to outbluff the Chinese and threatened to bomb the Chinese mainland. What could President Truman do but fire him? Since Russia now had the hydrogen bomb, the stockpile grew, multiplying by the thousand, enough to level this whirling planet again and again.

Oppenheimer told us, as Einstein had done, "The atomic clock ticks faster and faster."

So the war ended on July 27, 1953, neither won nor lost. Eisenhower seeking election had promised "Peace with Honor"—one more cliché for our long list of political slogans. Nobody called it that as we stumbled out of war with Korea in an uneasy truce. At least Stalin was dead, a brutal dictator for twenty-nine years. But it was not peace. It was a cease-

fire, not for good, for the time being. To paraphrase Dryden:
Our wars brought nothing about, our lovers were all untrue.

David graduated from Harvard in June, 1952, in wartime.
Commissioned by the Navy with the rank of ensign, he was
assigned immediately to active duty on a destroyer with the
Sixth Fleet, the USS *Beatty*, which had only just returned
from Korean waters where it had been under fire.

In every sense of the terrible word his ship was a destroyer
—built for the purpose, a tight, swift weapon of war meant
primarily to track down and destroy submarines. During
David's three years of service on the *Beatty*, where they
made him an officer of antisubmarine and torpedo warfare,
they tried to make him a destroyer too. He was hardly the
military type. He was under orders. They urged him to
become a career man in the Navy. But they failed.

Meanwhile we observed a family ritual or ceremony each
June, with somebody always graduating or getting married.
B. and I took the trip north to Cambridge with marvelous
festive regularity, the moment our school term was over.
We saw David married to Peggy in Harvard College Chapel
in 1953. We saw Philip graduated with Joan one day in
1954 and married to her in Harvard Memorial Church the
next.

Both sons chose to marry Radcliffe girls, from Ohio and
from Illinois, for much the same reason, I imagine, that B.
chose to marry me—for love and forever. Peggy was still in
her junior year when David returned on a twenty-day leave
to celebrate their wedding. Now he would have a wife waiting
for him at the dock. B. had to sign the license to permit Phil,
not yet twenty-one, to take a bride.

It was working out improbably well, enough to dash the
breath away: we had sons and daughters and no thankless
child.

When Philip decided upon Duke University that fall for graduate study in physics, he and Joan found a house in our own countryside, a couple of fields away, to become our neighbors. We gave them all our friends as part of the housewarming. When David was released from the Navy, he entered the Harvard graduate school to work for a Ph.D. in English. Our sons had been lucky in love and in war, like us. Their lives were happy, civilian, academic, and now for the first time utterly their own.

Then strange to say, a little too pat, a little too soon, the time seemed to have come for me to die. I couldn't agree it was the right time or poetically just, not like the departure of John Crowe Ransom's lady who died so gracefully of fever and chills, surrounded by love,

> The delight of her husband, her aunts, an infant of three,
> And of medicos marvelling sweetly on her ills.

Yet the headlong fact presented itself as if on schedule, and room must be made for it. Not the survival of the planet but my own survival was in doubt—the cosmic joke was on me. Though I could have used more time to grow mellow and beneficent, not to lose but to find myself, this was my fortune and fortune was outrageous. I appeared to be fatally ill.

The surgeon who performed what was expected to be a minor operation, requiring an overnight stay in hospital, removed a small lump near my left armpit. He had to inform B. of the result. The growth was malignant.

B. said, "How shall I tell her?"

"You won't have to tell her," he said. "She'll know."

I came up from a black well of unconsciousness. And I knew. It was only some days later I decided upon suicide. That is, after the unspeakable massive pain, the humiliation of begging like a whimpering child for the hypodermic needle, the single desire for oblivion, the mounting awareness of how terribly, slowly, surely one could be destroyed, I said to myself, "I refuse." Such a vow a prisoner might swear who expected to make his escape this time, for a little while. The prognosis was not good enough —there was the nearness to the lymph glands, and there was the delay. *The delay.*

Several months before, B. and I had skidded in our Chrysler on a slippery road and plunged down a steep embankment. B. was shaken up but unhurt. Because the seat beside him was a folding seat, built to push forward in a two-door sedan, I was thrown with violent force against the gearshift, which plunged into my armpit. For weeks the pain was intense, unlocalized, as if my rib cage had been broken. Then the one spot stayed hurt, painful to touch, a swelling.

Two doctors and the surgeon who operated thought it unlikely the accident had anything to do with the lump that developed there. They dismissed it as probably a coincidence, though the prolonged soreness was unusual. I suppose they knew or made a reasonable guess. But because of it I waited, did not act. There was the delay. Any fault was my own.

On the afternoon B. brought me home from the hospital, over a cocktail I looked into his face and told him my simple plan. It needed no elaborating or justifying, seeming so obvious an answer, as a last resort, that I expected him to agree—how could he not? He knew I preferred to live. He would understand the rest, that I refused to let him see me descend into agony from which there was no return. Anybody would refuse, given the choice.

B. was an understander. No one was easier to tell the truth to, or hear the same from in return. Besides, by being so well married we were of a like mind. He listened without a word, calm and thoughtful, and heard me out. To my bewilderment he shook his head: *no,* he did not agree. No, he said, no. It wasn't logical or rational, it made no sense. I wasn't thinking clearly; there were maggots in my brain. No one was free to take his own life. Life had to be lived on whatever terms, no matter what the cost. It was the price one paid for existence. Nothing gave one the right to toss it away, *nothing.*

"You see this as a kind of reckoning, in black and white. Oh, my love, my love. Wait a little. Wait till you're well again."

I thought: he doesn't believe me. He can't. It hasn't happened to him. I was listening to a different drummer.

So we dropped the subject, never in our lives to refer to it, to speak a word further. Soon we were laughing over a second cocktail, talking of less mortal events. It was a miracle to be home.

Since the operation came two weeks before Christmas, I managed with the intervening holidays to miss only five rounds of classes, which B. taught for me. I could return to work with my pride intact, as if the vault of sky hadn't fallen. But the time was limited to now, without past or future, suspended as far as the end of my nose.

During the spring term, I wrote a great deal on my free days. Nothing so occupied the mind. The verses were light, lighter than ever, as they had to be. It was too late in my life to begin to speak with sobriety. I knew no sober words for love and death, or how to write an amusing piece for the *New Yorker* entitled "Waiting." One had to sweat out the waiting for as long as five years, I heard. My surgeon said, "Longer than that."

Yet why not hope? By the middle of summer, with six months of health behind me and the habit of living, the idea gradually faded a little. With fingers crossed, I began to feel restored to this world. Perhaps I had been morbid, perhaps death was only a maggot in my brain. I went to see Dr. Anders in July for a routine checkup.

"We're going to London again in September, Bev and I," I said during the examination. "Can you recommend a doctor for me to see over there?"

He glanced at me sharply. "London? For how long?"

"For the year. Bev wants to finish some research. I have a sabbatical leave coming up at last."

He turned to his calendar. "September. Two months away. If you don't mind, I'm going to put you back in hospital first." To his nurse he said, "See how soon a private room is available and reserve it for her."

I sat up on the examining table. "What did you find?" I said.

"Nothing much."

"You found something."

"Not exactly. Let's say I'm worried; it doesn't look too sure. We both know the danger exists. As a precaution, a safety measure, I want to try another operation, a slightly more radical one on your breast. It won't be any worse than last time. It may help. You'll soon be able to travel, and I'll feel a lot better about letting you leave the country for a whole year."

The word he used was *pre-cancerous*.

I said: "I refuse."

Dr. Anders stared at me in silence. "It's my life," I said. He turned and walked out of the consulting room.

So we were back, as Frost said, in the middle of March. This time it was providential to be going away to England. Had I believed in Providence, I should have seen its benign hand in the devising of this clever plan.

I had hated leave-takings before, most of all leaving my children. This time I might be unreturning; I didn't expect to see them again. On the other hand one always had these dark premonitions at parting. This time the fact I was taking along a bottle of 120 Seconal pills was of little relevance—a private matter I had to solve alone.

We had rented our house for the year to a visiting professor and his wife from the University of Liège. It was September, 1955. The morning paper said, "Duke's Bevingtons off for England" (sounding like a dance band), and off we went, first to Massachusetts, where David and Peggy had taken an apartment on Oxford Street, Cambridge. They had brightened it with yellow paint and hung a big Matisse print in the dining room. Peggy herself lit up a room like Juliet. I loved them for being happy. I loved David for joking in farewell: "We feel like a middle-aged couple sending their adored children off to boarding school."

As we left the New York harbor on the *Parthia* bound for Liverpool, Philip and Joan were standing at the dock to say goodbye, laughing and waving in the highest spirits. The three quick blasts of the departing ship cried, "I love you, love you, love you." But Phil wrote us in London: "Somehow I think I minded this parting more than any other."

For a week before we moved back to our favorite London lodging, the Hotel Sandringham in Hampstead, we were invited to stay at Harkness House, 35 Portman Square, a house given over to the furthering of Anglo-American understanding. It was a lovely old mansion (connected I think with the English-Speaking Union) whose goodwill mission it was to bring Americans closer to the English, or the other way round, and lessen the strain.

The sole request made of the few guests who could be accommodated at one time—dons, professors, Commonwealth scholars, writers—was that they consent to breakfast together. The warden of Harkness House, Mr. S. Gorley Putt, presided each morning at the coffee urn and encouraged an exchange of views.

It was a bold plan at a bad moment when Americans were increasingly unpopular in England. The frostbitten *New Statesman and Nation* made it their policy to be hostile and rude, deploring us with a shudder in each issue. On October 28, the B.B.C. network broadcast a debate by the Oxford Union of Oxford University, whose motion was: "This House regrets the example and influence of the United States of America." The affirmative won hands down. Hating Americans had become a national pastime. Personally I couldn't understand it. I've always liked Americans (even though Churchill called us an unfathomable mixture). At least at Harkness House they tried to improve relations and keep us cousins if not brothers by getting us off to an early, inspiriting start.

Our first night there, the other couple staying in the house was Mr. and Mrs. C. P. Snow, passing through London on their way to Italy for a holiday. At breakfast they proved the most bearable of company, conversable, warm, and attentive, so friendly that by a second cup of coffee I had launched upon an extended eulogy, if not magnification, of Mr. Snow's works, which I admired. I spoke highly of *The Light and the Dark,* praised *The Masters,* applauded *The Search,* grew lyrical over *Time of Hope.*

Mr. Snow listened enrapt, as well he might to such laudatory remarks, after which he replied with modest gratification. It seemed to me we were not only improving Anglo-American relations, we were already hand in glove. With a pleased smile and a sweep of the arm, he pointed to the lady beside him.

"This is my wife," he said.

154

The abrupt change of subject was startling. Nobody had questioned for an instant his being married or expressed a doubt that this was the lady he was married to. Besides, she had been introduced an hour earlier as Mrs. Snow. I smiled cordially across the table at her and she smiled back. We were all smiles.

"Pamela Hansford Johnson," added Mr. Snow.

It was a tense moment, a time for someone to break in with a tactful remark, a time if ever for diplomacy between nations. Mr. Putt, where was your hand across the sea? A sepulchral silence fell.

"How do you do," I murmured into my plate.

"How do you do," said Pamela Hansford Johnson.

After breakfast we hurried to Foyle's to buy her novels (not all fifteen!), and by nightfall I had finished *Girdle of Venus* and made a start on *An Impossible Marriage*. Too late. At breakfast next morning the C. P. Snows were gone, quite gone, on their way to write another book apiece and bask in the Italian sun.

At the Hotel Sandringham, under new management with young Mr. Dreyer as proprietor and his pretty wife as cook, we were given our old room, No. 12, the (unredecorated) bridal suite and the same view of spires of chimneypots to the dome of St. Paul's. It had the air and aspect of home, if one thinks of home as a precipice. Nothing had changed (had it?) except that now we were returning to old haunts— the Heath, the autumn mists, the Coach and Horses with its tepid beer, its red roses, its sign COURAGE (which I had not got), the three jolly Turtons, the same faces at the bar. On a night of swirling fog they seemed like people adrift in a perilously small lifeboat.

"Stay here," said Mr. Dreyer. "You are with friends." This was, in fact, our third stay at the Hotel Sandringham, since in the summer of 1952 we had come to London bringing Philip, while David on naval duty attended Fleet Sonar School at Key West—sonar, for detecting submarines.

England had become a habit. By now we had traveled in each of its counties, and I had written about Cowper's rabbits in Olney, Emily Brontë's moors at Haworth, Herrick in Devon, Wordsworth in Alfoxden, Mr. White in Selborne, the man from Porlock, and Caxton of Kent; about the room at the George Inn, Salisbury, where Pepys slept with his wife on a Wednesday, June 10, 1668, and I slept with B. a hundred thousand nights later; about the jackdaws in Bedfordshire, the swans at Wapping Old Stairs, the geraniums in the bomb sites, the time at Greenwich, the lovers in Hyde Park, the red roses at the pub, the Heath misty with poems; about Everlasting Lane, St. Albans, which had proved with the passing of years so short it was now being extended.

B. really loved London, a city man at heart unspoiled by his own green meadows. He preferred fleshpots to flowerpots. My mother wrote, "Next time I expect to hear you have moved to London for the rest of your life."

She was wrong. It was *this* time I had come for the rest of my life.

On the night of October 22, we went to a meeting at Central Hall, Westminster, to hear Bertrand Russell speak against war and for world peace. He was an old acquaintance, too. As I listened in the packed auditorium to his railing words—an angry old man trying to save an unsavable world—I had to laugh to recall the last time we'd met. On a Saturday morning in early September, three years before, Josephine the chambermaid at the Sandringham had wakened us by a knock at the door and, opening it, dropped a curtsy that for a hefty woman took a while to execute. "Lord Russell is on the tellyphone," she gasped.

He called to ask us to spend the day with him at his home on Queen's Road, Richmond, as the year before during a lecture tour he had visited us in North Carolina. Philip had gone off for a fortnight in France. B. and I arrived in Richmond near lunchtime. It was one of the happiest days of my life.

The extraordinary pleasure was his company. At eighty, Bertrand Russell lived alone on the two upper floors of a rambling old house occupied on the lower floors by his son John, Viscount Amberly, his son's wife, and three little children. We were left undisturbed to talk all day. Only the cook appeared briefly to lay the table and serve lunch. For tea we drank sherry. In the late afternoon we took an hour's brisk walk in Richmond Park that he might show us Pembroke Lodge, where he lived with his grandparents from the age of four after his parents' early death.

The stately house surrounded by rose gardens was now a tearoom, closed in September with the end of summer, its doors locked and bolted. Cupping our hands against the panes, we three trespassers peered through dusty windows at the piled-up tea tables while he described how it used to look when Gladstone came to tea—the Victorian drawing rooms with their heavy bric-a-brac (including a large marble statue of a naked lady), their aged occupants and famous visitors like the Shah of Persia and Queen Victoria; his schoolroom, now filled with thick crockery and tea-urns; his lost world of seventy-five years ago.

Anyone might well regret such a loss of empire, but he appeared not to. Thinking of a past visible before us, forever usurped, I asked the idiotic question, "Are you a sentimental man?"

"Quite sentimental," he said, smiling as we walked away.

And I think he was. Bertrand Russell loved Shelley, for example (yet hated Wordsworth), because his grandfather

Lord John Russell had been born in the same month and year as Shelley and that date linked him with the Romantics. He rejected T. S. Eliot, who had been his student and friend, because Eliot joined the church. It pleased me to find the most authentically great man I ever met capable of such unashamed caprice.

But his wit was an enormous pleasure, with his barking laugh to signal a just appreciation of it. He may have lacked humility but not wit. Age had no grip on him. He believed himself still very much a man (the prime of Bertrand Russell) and so he was, an uncommon stayer—neither wizened like a prune nor tired nor forgetful. I envied him his sure hold on longevity.

Back in his rooms, our gaiety combined and multiplied as, smoking his eternal pipe, he described the books he was writing, among them his autobiography while the yesterdays remained, not to be published till after his death. From the scandalous tales he then told, or read aloud from manuscript (of his consuming love affair with willowy Lady Ottoline Morrell, whose hair was the color of marmalade and who must have been twice the height of this skinny little man), I thought to myself such revelations might wait till the twenty-second century. Clearly his intentions in the matter were good, those of an honest philosopher with no plan to live forever or proceed from there to the life everlasting. Yet by the age of ninety-seven, either his patience wore thin or he began to feel posthumous, for in that year (1969) the *third* volume of these memoirs in all their nakedness appeared.

I liked the way he ended his autobiography, ". . . the world, for all its horrors, has left me unshaken," both because it was so defiant a claim and because it was demonstrably untrue.

On his doorstep at dusk, as we were bidding him goodbye,

Bertrand Russell took me in his arms and kissed my mouth with what might be described as passionate civility. So startled was I by this salute, bestowed with abandon by a perfect and obliging host, that B. had to lead me away glassy-eyed and speechless, guiding me in a trance reeling down the steps, steering us both in the direction of the train station. B. laughed as he hauled me along, then sighed in admiration. "What a *man*," he said.

All this I recalled the night of the mass meeting in Westminster, without wanting in the least a repetition of it. Bertrand Russell's new wife sat on the platform with him, an attractive, sensible woman, doubtless a sympathetic one. He spoke brilliantly, fearlessly, as one dedicated to the survival of the human race on this planet for whom his hopes had grown dim. "Is man to renounce war or choose universal death?" he stormed. Man was too crafty to be saved even by an expert. Russell would die someday in the attempt. I wondered (in case I outlived him) if I would grieve for him when he was dead, and I knew I would, but more perhaps for myself and for mankind. Out of pity he besought man's humanity to man, and it was too much to ask. We were children lost in a wood. He couldn't show us the way out.

When the ovation was over, B. and I left the hall without making ourselves known.

We had tickets to the British Museum Reading Room, old customers, where B. went every weekday to work from nine to five. I chose to stay in our hotel room, like the Hermit of Hampole, and write beside the gasfire (feeding it shillings at a ruinous rate), partly because I was trying to finish a third book of verse, partly because it was a convenient place to die, if I had to die.

The book, already accepted for publication in May by Houghton Mifflin, still lacked a title. I could imagine it appearing as ————and *Other Poems,* and so could its exasperated editor, Paul Brooks, who wrote by every other post, *"What* are we going to call it?" When I suggested by cable *The Starlings of Trafalgar Square,* Paul fired back word that he loathed starlings. The residents of the Sandringham then held a hasty conference chaired by the Latin teacher and came forward with two solutions: *Amid the Alien Corn* or *Faery Lands Forlorn,* they didn't care which. Desperate for time, I decided on *A Change of Sky,* dedicated it to Philip and Joan, and sat down to write a verse to justify and clarify the title.

The phrase echoed a line of Horace (I was ever an echoer): *Caelum, non animum mutant, qui trans mare currunt,* which has had many interpreters. Andrew Wood translated it: " . . . those who cross the sea change not their mind but climate only." Philip Francis wrote: "Not their own passions but the climate change." George Trevelyan took a look at *animum* and said: "They change their sky who travel far, but not their soul."

From the mind to the passions to the soul, the next step was easy to the heart. Systole and diastole. The meaning it had for me was personal, yet clear enough: "The sky is changed. I have not changed my heart."

For one other reason we had come to London: to visit the Queen (Mother). B. had been invited to represent Duke University at the Convocation of Her Majesty Queen Elizabeth the Queen Mother as Chancellor of the University of London. We both dreaded having to attend, since in America a convocation is a tedious affair of academic procession and droning set speeches. In England it swung into a wingding—two days and nights of stunning pageantry with lots of champagne.

Early in November we received notice of coming revelry

together with hints on court etiquette. The celebration would start on Wednesday, November 23, with a formal dinner at Bedford College and a reception to honor the lady at the Senate House. On Thursday, November 24 (Thanksgiving, as it happened), the installation would occur at the Royal Festival Hall, followed by a luncheon in Guildhall given by the Lord Mayor, followed by a dinner given by the Provost of University College, followed by a reception given by the Queen Mother at St. James's Palace. By that time we should be calling her by her first name. The rules of order were: formal evening dress "and decorations" (a Phi Beta Kappa key?) both evenings, the ladies to avoid black gowns but wear white kid gloves to the shoulder. Unrehearsed foreign visitors need not bow or curtsy. One waited for the Queen to speak first.

B. rushed me to Bond Street and himself picked out a Nina Ricci gown from Paris, a gold-threaded brocade like Julia's petticoat, "As airy as the leaves of gold," with sweeping skirt and matching coat—so elegant and tight in the waist that both B. and Mr. Dreyer (who looked upon the affair as adding pomp, prestige, and glory to his hotel) worked with a pair of pliers to zip me into it.

The week before, B. and I had practiced mingling with royalty when Alan Pryce-Jones asked us to lunch at his house in Cavendish Close with the Prince and Princess of Hesse. Why he did so I don't know. Perhaps since Alan had failed earlier to show us a poet, he wished to make amends by showing us a prince. Either choice was satisfactory, though no poet could have been more hilarious company or in better form.

The Prince, a great-grandson of Queen Victoria, was said to look remarkably like her, a fact of enormous advantage to him socially. At any moment in the lively talk, he might draw down the corners of his mouth to become the severe old

lady with dewlaps and widow's peak; and no matter what
one was about to say one would burst into laughter. I
wondered why he hadn't been offered the part in *Victoria
Regina*.

We told him of the great-grandson of Gladstone living in
Hampstead (since it seemed only fitting the two of them
should meet and exchange imitations). But the Princess, a
spontaneous and impulsive lady, dashed me by asking innocently, "Oh, you've taken a house for the season in *Hampstead?*"

The festival at Royal Festival Hall was, said the *Times,*
the finest show of academic magnificence the world has ever
seen. It was a cautious understatement. A pride of 140 distinguished professors and scholars came from the four corners
of the earth—from Russia (the rector of Moscow University),Greece, Israel, Poland, Tasmania, the Gold Coast, the
United States with no fewer than thirty delegates, and so on.
They came in robes of many colors, in velvet gowns of
bright green, pink, purple, deep yellow, with great squashy
doctors' caps or here and there a cloak and plume. Since the
academic dress of the University of London is fire red, the
hall was aflame with these professors; since the Lord Mayor
of London and the Lady Mayoress attended in medieval
costume of red and gold, the splash and glitter outdid a
carnival.

From my seat in the fifth row behind the Lord Mayor, I
kept one eye on B. marching chin up to "The Earl of
Oxford's March" as the procession moved to seats on the
platform, and one eye on Princess Margaret in a royal box
over my head, far from downcast after her recent rejection of the love of Group Captain Peter Townsend.
(The Queen had absented herself from what was strictly
her mother's party.) Margaret wore a royal-blue velvet coat
and feathered hat. B. walked with the Americans, who in
sober black gowns and squares—the English word—looked

gravely impressive, with just a fanciful touch of color in their hoods to give the nod to this royal masquerade.

Next came the modish ladies-in-waiting and gentlemen-in-waiting, slightly ill at ease as if bidden to the wrong fashion show, taking their seats on a platform banked with chrysanthemums. To a fanfare of trumpets, sounded by eight Royal Horse Guard trumpeters with gold-laced tunics and blue velvet caps, the Queen Mother advanced slowly down the center aisle. The Queen Mum, Mr. Dimbleby of the B.B.C. called her, as if she were a prize chrysanthemum. Her mortarboard had a gold edge and tassel, her black silk robe was aglisten, trimmed, frogged, and bordered with gleaming gold. She wore long white gloves and black pumps with high heels. A page in scarlet carried her train. I sensed her quick breathing as she passed, inches away, leaving a whiff of perfume very feminine for a lady scholar.

"May it please your Majesty . . . " the show began, and with a second fanfare Her Majesty sat down. Her chair was like a throne in the center of the stage. Her bearing was regal. Under the academic gown she wore a light-blue dress and a double strand of pearls. She gave a slight tug at her skirt to be sure her knees were covered.

This was splendid pageantry in the grand style. But the wit was extra and unexpected—at least I don't recall a display of wit at academic functions before. Even the Queen worked a little into her gentle address to the assembly. In praising the University of London as first in England to grant degrees to women, first to appoint a woman professor, first to elect a woman Vice-Chancellor, she added:

"Today, as you see, it has taken yet a further step. I thought you might wish me to direct your attention to an attitude so progressive."

I wished the Strachey sisters were on hand to hear and hurrah.

The Provost, Sir Ifor Evans, was as urbane as a

toastmaster in presenting the six notables to receive honorary degrees, commending the High Commissioner of India, Mrs. Pandit (Nehru's sister) for her skill as a cook; the Marquis of Salisbury for his foxy conduct in the House of Lords; the Lord Bishop of London for his fondness for the movies.

The bewigged barrister sitting next to me wept openly when Mrs. Pandit knelt on a stool before the Queen to be granted the degree of Doctor of Laws. No doubt the sense of occasion overcame him. Or it may have struck him as a glorious moment of English history, though the tableau hardly resembled Queen Victoria, Empress of India, bestowing an honor on a loyal subject. The Queen Mother spread her arms and with tender care placed the doctor's hood over Mrs. Pandit's uncovered head, then patted, smoothed, and adjusted the hood with a critical eye to be sure it fitted neatly. The two rare women stood beaming at each other and shook hands.

We ended by singing a lusty "God Save the Queen"—both Queens, I guess. Her Majesty departed as she had come, to the flourish of a trumpet sonata by Purcell.

At the Guildhall, B. and I sat at a table for two on the balcony between Gog and Magog, overlooking the banquet table below. So here we were above the salt. The Lord Mayor was a jaunty figure of a man, not old or portly, a becoming luncheon companion for the Queen Mother, who appeared gratified. We ate breast of pheasant off gold plate, which I should be glad to do every day. But it was the national custom of proposing toasts in frolic wine I found most estimable and entertaining.

How the English keep sober or upright at such feastings I wonder. Then and afterward at the Provost's dinner, we began by drinking the healths of the royal family, soon losing count, summoned to our feet time and again. God save royalty. God save winebibbers. As the racket increased at the state dinner that night, it became impossible to hear above the din what genial toast was being proposed to whom. The waiters refilled our wine glasses. We rose and sat, rose and sat.

An Englishman across the table giggled helplessly as he and I stood facing each other, glass at the ready. "Sit down, my girl! *Sit down,*" he said. "This time I'm toasting *you,*" meaning this libation was meant for the foreign visitors.

A thousand guests gathered at St. James's turreted and battlemented Palace, of whom the Queen Mother received the foreign guests privately, two by two. At 9:00 P.M. we formed a graceful queue up the staircase to the State Apartments where the reception was held. B. and I followed behind Mrs. Pandit, who bowed in greeting. She was accompanied by an Indian lady blinding in splendor in a scarlet and gold sari, a caste mark on her forehead, glittering diamonds in her hair, ears, and nose. Mrs. Pandit wore a pale-blue gown and no jewels. With her dark eyes and calm beauty she was the loveliest woman in the procession.

Of the full-length portraits along the great staircase, one was of Charles II in full regalia. He was the king who kept his many mistresses housed in St. James's Palace, creating for them the "Grace and Favour" apartments. He kept his spaniels at the Isle of Dogs and his pelicans in St. James's Park. Nowadays the apartments were available overnight as a place for the Poet Laureate to lay his head. If necessary, accommodations could be found for the Keeper of the Queen's Swans.

At the head of the staircase we filed with propriety and elegance through the Armoury among flashing shields and spears, beyond that to the narrow Tapestry Room. Here the Queen Mother received us. As B. and I were announced and entered alone, she stood waiting as if only for us, reaching out to clasp our hands. I had not seen the like—such bedecked radiance, such grace, such a pink-and-white sweet-pea complexion, or so many precious jewels outside the Tower of London. As Sir Philip Sidney said of another lady, "She was a Queen, and therefore beautiful."

Primed by a gentleman-in-waiting, she spoke her greeting: she had received an honorary degree from Columbia University and took pride in the honor that linked us. I trembled at so congenial a subject for fear B. would halt in his tracks and settle down for an hour's chat. After a moment we managed to move on into the state rooms with their thousand guests and waiters bearing trays of champagne. An inaudible string orchestra was composed of Grenadier Guards.

It was lovely wandering through the Queen Anne Room, Council Chamber, Throne Room, Art Gallery with B., who was good at spotting celebrities—the Princess Royal, Princess Alice, the Prime Minister Anthony Eden—each lending a touch of cosmos. It was delightful stopping to talk with American friends, till, all at once, I knew I had to sit down. Either the party or the champagne had gone to my head; more likely, because of the tight gown I had stopped breathing. I excused myself and wobbled off in search of a chair, an item altogether missing in the furnishings of a palace. A voice from behind me said quietly, "My dear, you're very pale. Come, sit here with me. Come, I insist."

A handsome white-haired man with crutches beside him motioned me to the small bench against the wall. He took my pulse and wiped the beads of sweat from my brow. He put his arm around me and kept it there.

"Hold your head down," he said. "You're about to faint. Lean against me and try to relax. It's quite proper, I'm a medical doctor, you know."

He was also Principal and Vice-Chancellor of Capetown University, South Africa. Having fallen in love with him on the spot, I gladly stayed, even after B. found me. And that was how we came to meet Clement R. Attlee and the Earl of Athlone. Everyone, it seemed, knew this courtly gentleman, Mr. T. B. Davie, and sought him out as an old friend. He didn't attempt to rise nor did I, with my head under his chin. It was only afterward I discovered how well known, how beloved, a man he was in England. That was by reading with grief a month later the long obituary of him in the London *Times*.

Like Yeats I had met in my life some beautiful lofty people. It looked as if the gods had arranged these recent excursions and lordly pleasures for my benefit. They softened the blow with benevolence. They were giving me a big sendoff, prolonging my departure, since by December 10 I had lived the year through, a great loiterer. I wished I could rejoice as Pepys did on each anniversary of his cutting, who "did resolve while I live to keep it as a festival" and kept the stone itself in a jewel case that cost him 25s.

I forget now with any clarity how it felt to be without expectation of survival. However it was, it is untellable. And however it was, here I still am alive on this earth. I don't know the depths I reached, only that they were intermittent. What I lost was not hope so much as anticipation of tomorrow, a feeling the British had known daily during the years of the blitz. It hadn't happened to me yet. It might not happen. I was, in Dryden's words, "half seas o'er to death."

But that it stayed in my mind, unbanished, with some sinking of the heart, I know from memories like these—the noting of the exact time when Josephine finished her morning work on the third floor so that I would be uninterrupted the rest of the day. The hoarded pills. The search of my flesh for a fatal sign. The aimless solitary walks on the Heath. The fascination of watching people as they boarded the bus to Golders Green, the district just north of Hampstead. That was where the crematorium was.

I often wondered what I thought death to be. The answer came out ever the same: death was nothingness. Death was not being, totally not being. It was an end with no afterwards. A poor choice.

For bolstering the hours I read books as sustainers: Montaigne, who said we are all novices at this business of death. "My art and my profession is to live." They were curative words, written unfortunately by a dead man.

I read Wallace Stevens, who had died six months before:

> The house was quiet because it had to be.
>
> The quiet was part of the meaning, part of the mind:
> The access of perfection to the page.
>
> And the world was calm.

The house and the world were the same thing. And they were not quiet after all, and they were not really calm. It was only that they had to be.

"Give me life," said Falstaff.

Vivamus, mea Lesbia.

I read with care Camus's *Myth of Sisyphus,* his tale of Absurd Man condemned during the preposterous brevity of life to roll his heavy stone to the top of the mountain and as it tumbled down roll it up without knowing why, again, again, again. Camus had written the book to resolve for himself, if he could, the problem of suicide. He wanted to discover its logic and its integrity. "Is one to die voluntarily or to hope in spite of everything?" Yet he hadn't succeeded in stating the problem for me, or if he had I didn't understand it. Life seemed to me not absurd to start with, ironic but not absurd, since I passionately assented to it. Nor did the plight of Sisyphus need justifying ("One must imagine

Sisyphus happy"). I, Sisyphus, was happy. Existence had plenty of meaning, and the meaning was love. My refusal was not to live, far from it. It was a refusal to submit to being senselessly destroyed.

That plight, so far as I could see, was not covered by the book.

At the same time I studied Spanish to please B., since he had decided to take us for a European holiday on the first of March (exactly as we had done six years before), and this time to travel in Spain. Each night at teatime he gave me a vocabulary test, groaning over my unparalleled ignorance. He at least had a reading knowledge of the language.

"Darling, how many meager words do you actually know in Spanish?" he asked.

"*Mañana*. I know *mañana* and *nada*. *Mañana nada*."

"That won't get you far in Spain. How many more?"

I counted on my fingers. "Five."

"After two months of study you can't tell me in Spanish which is your left hand and which your right?"

"I can quote Cervantes."

"Go ahead."

"*Digo, paciencia y barajar*. Patience, and shuffle the cards."

Mr. Dreyer tapped lightly on the door of our room. It was three o'clock in the morning.

"A telephone call for you. It's from America," he said. "You can take it in my office."

B. leaped out of bed and was ahead of me down the stairs, since he didn't bother to throw on a robe. When I arrived followed by Mr. Dreyer, B. was shouting to the operator, and fear rasped his voice. For what seemed five minutes he waited for the connection. Then "Yes," he said, and louder "Yes, *yes!*" He was listening.

He was weeping, the tears splashing down his face. "Philip," he said, the one choked word, and when I grabbed his arm he motioned me to be quiet so that he could hear. Was he talking *to* Philip? Had Philip called to tell us some terrible news of David? Or was it David at the other end trying to explain some terrible thing that had happened to Philip? It had to be one or the other. No other thought occurred to me. One son or the other.

"Philip?" I whispered. B. nodded his head.

"Is he dead?"

Incredibly, B. weeping asked the same question into the phone. "Is he *dead?*" By his ashen face I couldn't be sure. All he said was, "We're flying home as soon as we can get there. We'll take the first flight out, tonight if possible."

Mr. Dreyer had opened the telephone book to look up the number of the London airlines.

B. hung up the phone. "My God, my God."

At midnight on March 1, twenty-one hours later, B. and I were three miles high over London on our way home. Our plane, fantastically named "The Rainbow," was many hours late, delayed by bad weather in its flight from Brussels. We watched the lights dim and flicker out along the British coast. Ahead in the blackness lay the Atlantic Ocean and, if one could hold on that long, New York beyond, the airport at Idlewild. . . .

Abruptly the pilot was speaking, his words blurred and unclear. Iceland, I thought he said. He paused, then repeated the words more distinctly. Because of eighty-mile headwinds, we would take a northerly direction, following the coast upward to the North Atlantic. We had changed course and were on our way to Iceland. *Iceland?*

The nightmare day had passed without further word of Philip. It might mean anything—that he was still alive, that he was not alive. We knew no more than Dr. Nielsen had told last night by telephone. He was Philip's chairman at Duke, a taciturn man and partially deaf, not a man to offer false hope. At noon yesterday after a physics lecture, Philip had accepted a ride in a friend's new Volkswagen. The little car had gone out of control, slammed across the road, crashed into a tree. At the impact Philip's back was broken, the spinal cord severed. When they extricated him from the wreck and placed him in the ambulance, he was in shock, barely breathing, minutes from death. It had happened yesterday and this was almost tomorrow.

B. had found errands to do all morning in London, like canceling the rental of a car from the Godfrey Davis Company, the Morris Minor that was to have taken us to Spain. Like giving away the two tickets to *Waiting for Godot* we had expected to see tonight. After finishing the packing, I sat all day by the telephone or walked on the Heath—first one, then the other. Mr. Dreyer in his compassion chose not to tell the residents of our leaving. We wouldn't have to say goodbye.

I read again Phil's letter of a couple of days ago. He was scheduled to read his first paper shortly at the Washington meeting of the American Physical Society. "Life is going to be a little tough," he wrote. That was the way it was.

The bitter sleet and piercing cold greeted us in Iceland. We stepped from the plane at Reykjavik, slipping and stumbling on the glassy ice. Inside the airport for a cup of coffee, I glanced up at the clock on the wall. *Twelve o'clock!* I looked again. How could it say that? How could it possibly? We had left London at midnight. How in God's name could it be twelve o'clock *now?*

At that moment I became frantic. *What time was it?* It was no time at all! We were somewhere in the Arctic Circle and the clock had stopped, it stood still, we would never reach home. This was the end of the journey.

I turned to B. in terror. I pointed at the clock and opened my mouth to scream. He shook me to make me speak and, when he finally grasped the meaning of my panic, led me nearer to the clock to show me the sign beneath it: New York time.

"It's all right, love, Don't you see? It's midnight at *home*, not here. It's midnight where Philip is."

The night took a lifetime crossing the starless Atlantic, over a forever sea, enveloped in space. Yet it was hardly long enough to bring me to my senses. Let him live, I prayed to myself, over and over, let him live! Let him live *no matter what the cost.* Let him live *at any price.* Only give him the courage to go on living. I could imagine him paralyzed for life, even bedridden, even in constant pain, but I couldn't give him up. The only difference that mattered was the simple one between life and death.

For a while it didn't occur to me how much I asked, or that at least one question had answered itself. The question was no longer a matter of my own life. It was my son's. My own tremendous self-concern had at last been shocked from my mind. At last when I began to understand what his death would do to me, his unwilled death, *at last* I felt something like awareness, so late, of the hurt I could give to others. I knew my own cowardice.

For the first time, the logic that B. had understood, that Camus had struggled to explain, was clear. Or clearer. (But then Camus was to die four years later in a senseless car crash when the car he rode in as passenger hit a tree—the same accident as Philip's. B., my husband, was to die of cancer, a brain tumor, the kind of death I had been afraid to die. With courage that never failed him, without bargaining with mortality, he taught me how it was done. So what absurdity, what irony, of existence are we talking about?)

It was clear this night I had been cruelly mistaken, preoccupied with self, wilful and blundering. Philip had given me back my life, perhaps at the loss of his own. And from it the truth was becoming starkly defined: life must be lived, no matter what the terms. One could not take fate into one's own hands by a voluntary departure. One was not free to say, "I refuse."

I turned to B. and kissed him.

About noon our plane came down for a landing at Idlewild, and we went quickly through customs. B. and I raced along the corridor to the first telephone booth we could find. We called our neighbor Howard's number in Durham. He would be the easiest, the surest, to reach. He would know.

Howard answered the telephone. Not generally a taciturn man and certainly not a deaf one, this time he spoke without greeting or ceremony, wasting no words. It took only three.

"He will live," Howard said.

THE RETURN

Circling from out the sky we ribbon down,
As if in us were no anxiety,
At the lag end, to hurry the descent,

But rather a more lingering desire
To view the earth and air impartially,
As if we thrived in either element.

And yet, I am one transatlantic flier
Who looks with love on Idlewild below,
Frantic with longing on that beckoning strip,

Aflame to further the relationship.
I have been overnight how quick to learn
This desperate love, taught dearly in the sky,

This lusting for the world of roofs and trees,
Which we are skimming now so casually,
To which (but at a snail's pace) we *return!*